Dear Sarah

~

Life Letters To Help & Heal, With Love From Psychic Sarah

by

Sarah Delamere Hurding

Published by

Rainbow Wisdom

Copyright © 2017 Sarah Delamere Hurding

All rights reserved.
No part of this publication may be reproduced, stored in a retrieval system, or transmitted, in any form or by any means, electronic, mechanical, photocopying, recording or otherwise without the prior permission of *Rainbow Wisdom*

This book is sold subject to the condition that it shall not, by way of trade or otherwise, be lent, re-sold, hired out, or otherwise circulated without the publisher's prior consent in any form of binding or cover other than that in which it is published and without a similar condition including this condition being imposed on the subsequent purchaser. Names have been modified in the book to protect the identities of certain individuals. Others are included with full permission.

ISBN: 978-0-9997060-8-4

ABOUT THE AUTHOR

SARAH DELAMERE HURDING IS ONE OF IRELAND'S AND AMERICA'S BEST-KNOWN MYSTICS. A SEER, HEALER, LIFE COACH, WRITER, AUTHOR, ACADEMIC, FORMER CBS RADIO HOST AND WORLD PUJA NETWORK PRESENTER, OM TIMES FEATURED WRITER AND CONSCIOUSNESS FACILITATOR, SARAH BRINGS A FULL RANGE OF TALENTS TO THE TABLE.

Psychic Sarah is known for her accuracy, healing and manifesting abilities. Louis Walsh and Simon Cowell were stunned into silence when Sarah predicted the full line up of Irish Popstars SIX. She read for 32 talented kids and accurately named the final six. Sarah has also have been publicly recognised as an effective healer. She can lift pain with her hands pretty much instantly, and has helped clients with all kinds of issues and conditions. Her specialities are lifting pain and depression, as well as energy boosts, major clearings and resets using distance healing techniques. Once you sign up with Sarah, her commitment to you is relentless and strong. She works with you 24/7 with advice, guidance, energy, prayer and mutually agreed intentions for days, weeks and months depending on your needs.
Find Sarah at www.sarahdelamer.com

#mermaidmagic

Also by Sarah Delamere Hurding

StarScope

StarScope with Psychic to the Stars Sarah Delamere Hurding

Sarah correctly predicted the final line up of the pop band Six. Bono called her in when he was setting up his Kitchen nightclub at The Clarence, and according to Louis Walsh, she's "the woman who knows everything."
Now Ireland's top psychic has decided to share her gift in probably the only horoscope guide you will ever need to buy.
For the inside track on where your love, life, career and health are heading, keep this by your bedside.
Which celebrity shares your birthday? What lies ahead for you this year? Are you in the right relationship or are you and your partner completely incompatible? Are you in the right career?
Where should you go on holiday?

Get your life in balance with Sarah and *StarScope*
Published by *Poolbeg Ireland*.

To
Fred n' Mary

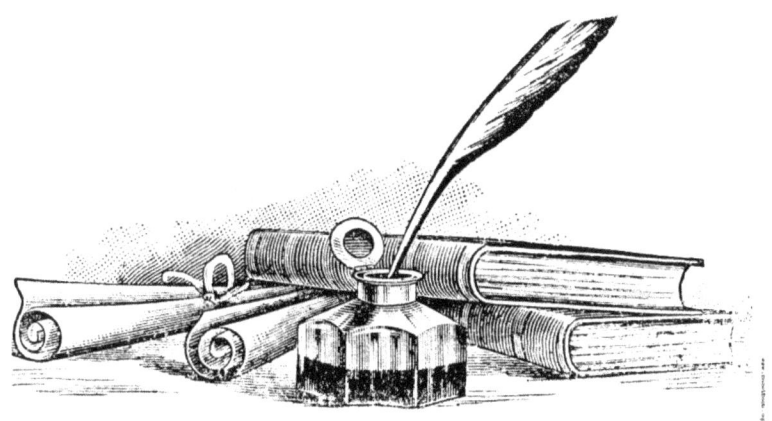

CONTENTS

Intention set for book 'Dear Psychic Sarah' with contact details. Page 14.

1) Introductory Chapter: What is psychic ability? Page 16.

2) Autobiographical note from psychic researcher, and spiritual healer Sarah Delamere Hurding. Page 25.

3) Aura Soma Colour healing system offers an alternative approach to our problems. All the letters contain a note, and recommendation of which Aura Soma bottle might help the situation. Page 29.

4) CHAPTER ONE: Psychic Ability – The Gift

   Letters:
   - Can I Learn To Be Psychic? Pages 33 - 34.
   - World Trade Centre. Pages 34 - 35.
   - Clairvoyant 'Gift'. Pages 37 - 38.
   - Can I Switch Off My Psychic Ability? Pages 38- 39.
   - Developing The 'Gift'. Pages 40 – 41.
   - Will I Win The Lottery? Pages 41 – 42.
   - Whom To Trust? Pages 43 - 44.
   - Misleading Information. Pages 44 – 45.
   - Mediumship. Pages 45 –46.
   - Confused Readings. Pages 47 –48.
   - Pop Star Fantasy? Pages 48 – 49.
   - Destiny: Can We Change It? Pages 50 – 51.
   - Are Tarot Cards Evil? Pages 52 – 53.
   - Is Fortune Telling Unreliable? Pages 53 – 54.
   - Draining Work Situation. Pages 54 – 55.

5) CHAPTER TWO: Good Luck/Bad Luck

   Letters:
   - Improving Your Luck. Pages 56 – 57.

- Winning Money. Pages 58 – 59.
- Bad Luck. Pages 59 – 60.

6) CHAPTER THREE: Psychic Finances

    Letters:
- Lottery Numbers. Page 62.
- Cursed Re Money? Page 64.
- Debt And Psychic Phone Readings. Pages 65 – 66.
- Making Money From Psychic Ability. Pages 66 – 67.
- Debt And Borrowing. Pages 67 – 68.
- Psychic Lotto Numbers. Pages 69 – 70.
- Silver Spoon Dilemma. Pages 71 – 72.
- Led Astray Financially? Pages 72 – 73.
- Legal Separation. Pages 74 – 75.
- Legacy Problem. Pages 75 – 76.

7) CHAPTER FOUR: Things That Go Bump In The Night

    Letters:
    Haunted House. Page 78 - 79.

8) CHAPTER FIVE: Eternal Triangles

    Letters:
- Love For Married Man. Page 80 - 81.
- Love Dilemma. Pages 82 - 83.
- Married Man. Pages 83 – 84.
- Wiccan Relationship. Pages 85 – 86.
- Unhappy Marriage. Pages 86 – 87.
- Affair Possibility. Pages 88 – 89.
- Destiny Moment. Pages 89 – 90.
- Affair Problem. Pages 91 – 92.
- Marriage To Gay Man. Pages 92 – 93.
- Betrayal And Loyalty. Pages 93 – 94.

9) CHAPTER SIX: Domestic Violence/Abuse

Letters:
- Aggressive Husband. Pages 95 – 96.
- Abusive Relationship. Page 97.
- Violent Abuse. Pages 98 – 99.
- Shall I Use The Gift? Pages 100 – 101.

10) CHAPTER SEVEN: Depression And Grief

Letters:
- How Do I Get A Life? Pages 102 -103
- Depression And Worry. Page 104.
- Depression. Pages 105 – 106.
- Obsessive Worry. Page 107.
- Preoccupation: Death/Cutting/Depression. Page 108.
- Letting Go. Pages 109 - 110.
- Bereavement. Pages 111 – 112.
- Clingy Co-Dependency. Pages 113 – 114.

11) CHAPTER EIGHT: Dilemmas

Letters:
- Moving Home. Pages 115 - 116.
- How People Change. Pages 117 - 118.
- Work Attraction. Pages 118 - 119.
- Kiss And Tell? Page 120.
- Moral Dilemma. Pages 121 – 122.
- Paternity Suit? Pages 123 – 124.
- Volatile Wife. Pages 125 – 126.
- Lack Of Fulfilment. Pages 126 – 127.

12) CHAPTER NINE: Career

Letters:
- Own Business? Page 128.
- Career And MS. Pages 128 - 129.
- What Next? Pages 130 – 131
- Russian Orthodox? Page 132.

13) CHAPTER TEN: Spiritual Landscape
    Letters:
- Name Changing. Page 133.
- Is Psychic Work Against God's Will? Page 134
- Political Deception. Pages 135 – 136.
- Catholicism And Readings. Page 137.
- Personal Development. Pages 139 – 140.
- Corrupt Priest. Pages 140 – 141
- Psychic Attack. Pages 142 – 143.
- Is Prediction Responsible? Page 144 – 145.
- Panic About Death. Pages 146 – 147
- Spiritual Money Spinning. Page 148.
- Developing Power. Page 149.
- Karmic Career. Page 150.
- Past Lives. Page 151.

14) CHAPTER ELEVEN: Relationships

    Letters:
- Waiting To Hear. Page 152.
- Romance. Pages 152 – 153.
- Commitment Issue. Page 153.
- Prison Release. Page 154.
- Love For Romance. Pages 155 – 156.
- Loneliness. Pages 156 – 157.
- Insecurity In Relationship. Pages 158 – 159.
- Confused Emotions. Pages 159 – 160.
- Failing Marriage. Pages 161 – 162.
- Lack Of Trust For Partner. Pages 162 – 163.
- Sister's Husband. Pages 164 – 165.
- Stifling Marriage. Pages 166 – 167.

15) CHAPTER TWELVE: Parenting and Family Ties

    Letters:
- Wayward son. Pages 167 - 168
- Holiday romance. Page 169.
- Worries re the future. Page 170.

- Family Problem. Pages 171 – 172.
- Parenting Issue. Pages 173 – 174.
- Parenting And Letting Go. Pages 174 – 175.

16) CHAPTER THIRTEEN: Soul Mate

   Letters:
   - Where Is My Soul Mate? Pages 176 – 177.
   - Teenage Angst. Page 178.
   - Desperation For Love. Page 179 – 180.
   - Love For A Pop Star. Pages 181 – 182.
   - Mixed Messages. Pages 183 – 184.

17) CHAPTER FOURTEEN: Unrequited Love

   Letters:
   - In Love With Counsellor. Pages 185 – 186.
   - Pregnancy Problem. Pages 187 – 188.
   - Powerful Attraction. Pages 188 – 189.
   - Endless Waiting. Pages 190 – 191.
   - Trapped By A Baby? Pages 191 – 192.
   - A Convenient Return. Pages 193 – 194.
   - Emotional Affair. Pages 194 – 195.

18) CHAPTER FIFTEEN: Media Issues

   Letters:
   - Pop Stars: Irish Style. Page 196 - 197
   - TV Work. Page 198 - 199.

19) CHAPTER SIXTEEN: Healing

   Letters:
   - Tony Quinn Seminar. Page 200 - 201
   - Shock And Panic. Page 202.
   - Failed Pregnancy. Page 203 - 204.
   - Living With Pain. Pages 205 – 206.
   - Drink Problem. Pages 206 – 207.

- Agoraphobia. Pages 208 – 209.
- Grief. Pages 209 – 210.
- Bereavement. Pages 210 – 211.
- Fertility. Page 211.
- Parenting And Personal. Pages 212 – 213.
- Nasty Fall. Page 214.
- Loss Of Mentor. Page 215.
- Pregnancy Success. Page 215.
- Thyroid Problem. Page 216.
- Suicidal Friend. Page 217.
- Panic Attacks /Message For All Readers. Page 219.

Dear Sarah

In this unusual book experienced psychic researcher Sarah Delamere Hurding covers a wide range of interesting subjects. It is a self–help book with a difference. The whole range of human problems is treated in an unusual and refreshing way. Without compromising anyone's privacy, Sarah explores a number of complex issues with unusual ease. Indeed a lot of the Book's content is vaguely autobiographical, which adds a personal touch to the advice given. If you become intrigued by Sarah's life story, her memoir Mermaid in The Kitchen is a real page turner.

Dear Sarah is designed to be accessible to all age groups of any ethnic background. Using an unusual mix of practical, spiritual and psychic advice Sarah brings a healing perspective to our suffering.

Because Sarah is a powerful healer and clairvoyant, you will find the process of reading the book a therapy in itself. Throughout the text Sarah makes reference to the properties of Aura Soma products and crystals. These offer another dimension to the questions raised. And suggest a means and alternative approach to tackling our problems. In a book that raises as many questions as it answers, Sarah is mindful of the responsibility of her work. This book may be read on many levels, so take from it what you will.

Many of the letters contained in the book are modifications or echoes of Sarah's own life experience. As such they present discreet autobiographical information presented with a view to help others. Along with letters from a selection of client's who have given permission, this book offers an unusual opportunity to understand the workings of all things psychic directly from a professional.

Any self-recognition in this work is entirely accidental, and does not refer directly to particular or identifiable situations. If you find yourself herein, it is simply a reflection of the universality of Sarah's psychic writing. It is the very reason the book is relevant. So do not panic.

Sit back and enjoy the ride!

Check out Sarah's web site www.sarahdelamer.com for further information.

Sarah welcomes your letters to email
sarahdelamerehurding@gmail.com

You may also make requests for healing to this address, and be assured the work is done for you. Make an appropriate donation to a charity of your choice. These letters will be treated with the utmost confidentiality.

What Is Psychic Ability?

In response to some of the more unfortunate representations of my work, I am grateful for this chance to explain myself. There are a lot of preconceived ideas about the psychic world, and the supposed mystics who haunt its corridors. Is the mystical profession an elaborate con, or are there genuine healers in circulation who can actually make a difference?

Unfortunately a great number of people, usually men I might add, view this phenomenon with a disinterested cynicism. It is as if such flaky ideas appeal immeasurably to their own sense of superiority. Sadly, they are by-passing a myriad of experience with such a restricted outlook. As with anything a bit of careful balance does not go amiss. Just as it is possible to give too much importance to a psychic reading, so too it is easy to get stuck in an endless maze of logic. We miss out on the subtle nuances of our lives by focusing relentlessly on the rational. What are the cynics afraid of - that there might be something in it? Perhaps the concept of someone being able to rummage through your psychic drawers is too much to bear.

By definition, a black and white reaction to life's diversity is limiting. The colour washes out of existence if we adhere too strongly to what makes sense. We all have - male and female alike - the propensity to think in a masculine or a feminine way. It is the feminine part of our psyche that connects with spiritual truth. Unless you're a rational fundamentalist of course! There are two gender-based reactions to life's realities.

The 'Macho' dismissive stifles thought with its rigidity and non-compromise; whilst gentle feminine openness is liberating and frees the mind. The truth is there are alternative ways of knowing and experiencing reality, which are equally valid and at times infinitely more enlivening than predictable cynicism. This is not to recommend that we lose the run of ourselves in endless flights of fancy, but spiritual awareness does open our eyes to different dimensions of perception.

Although science may no longer accept it as literally true, the concept of a left, and right side, to the brain is useful. Psychic ability accesses the creative part of the mind, usually referred to as right-sided brain function. It is this part of the mind that enables singers and authors to write, and journalists to come up with rather spooky headlines! Intuition and instinct play an important role, and it is their ability to listen to the small voice within that gives psychics the edge. We all have the capacity to recognise a gut feeling, and we all have a measure of psychic skill. This is one of the mind's faculties that may be developed.

Intuition is closely related to inspiration, and when the creative juices are flowing, a writer taps into the disconcerting experience of channelling. Comments like "That book just wrote itself" or "That song came to me after five minutes at the piano," are typical of material that comes from "nowhere." If you amplify this experience and add the skills of telepathy, and precognition you begin to unravel the mystery of psychic ability. The problem that left-brained thinkers have is no understanding of how secret and private information arrives in the lap of the psychic. Do these weirdos have inside knowledge? Do they know the people they are talking about? They surely must! How is it possible to comment on people you have never met?

The protestations of the cynics are ethically important. For a psychic working in the media, it is a delicate juggling act coming up with predictions about celebrities whilst preserving their right to privacy. I do try to monitor the phrasing of pieces, but it is a losing battle at times. Even certain things that I requested be off record have gone into papers, so apologies to anyone who has been offended. In general I feel comfortable predicting weddings, babies, and other happy events. However, this leaves me open to pushy journalists who want gory details. Sometimes I find myself in a position where I am aware of things that will occur, and yet I do not feel I can mention it. This is quite a pressure, but one that the cynics will love. I can hardly say I knew that something would happen after the event. Perhaps integrity is more important than always having to be right.

The other criticism that really riles me is that predictions are the result of intelligent guesswork. I would personally have no tolerance for communicating the calculations of my own mind. What use would I serve if all the insights I offer in good faith were merely contrivances of my own brain? To me there is no mystery in "knowing" things. It is a normal and integrated part of my life. Of course I can only speak for myself, but I am as genuine as I know how to be, and the catalogue of clients I have helped bears testament to this. Actually one of the most healing things someone can offer you is a good heart and a listening ear. Combine this with some psychic insight and things happen!

Legitimate psychic information comes from a variety of sources: the Akashic records; the universal unconscious or collective unconscious; angels and guides; and the psychic's own ability to interpret symbols. The Akashic records hold the details of our lives. They indicate our life's purpose, and the reasons for which we have been incarnated. There is a sense in which we all have an underlying awareness of what will happen to us. The psychic connects with this telepathically, and is thus able to read past, present, and future events.

Clairvoyance, clairaudience, and clairsentience all play a part in psychic interpretation. These faculties relate to the sensory experiences of seeing, hearing, and feeling. It is quite unusual for a psychic to have all these gifts in equal measure. Clairsentience is actually more common than clairvoyance. This would equate to a strong sense of knowing that comes from deep inside, which may be described as a powerful feeling that you don't have to question. Do not make the mistake of thinking that everything a psychic utters has its origin at this level. That would be dangerous indeed. Always retain a healthy scepticism – notice I did not say cynicism.

One of the problems with psychic interpretation is the timing of events. When you take into account that a "divine day" is supposed to be equivalent to a thousand of our years, you appreciate that the-powers-that-be, are not bothered if that job promotion is tomorrow or next year! Thankfully, I tend to get the age of a person at the time of significant events, which by passes the difficulty to an extent. However, it does not shift the reality that sometimes we have to accept that things will unfold in their own sweet time and not before. Knowing that something will happen is not the same thing as being able to influence it or bring it forward.

There is a huge responsibility that accompanies working professionally as a psychic and healer. It is one I do not take lightly. For a start it is quite daunting to go public'; not least because of the assumptions people make. I have experienced many forms of expectation directed at the work I do, and it is part of my pledge to work with honesty, integrity, and to the best of my ability. Someone said I was brave to stick my neck out by working with the media, and in a way that is true. I am a private person. However I do enjoy the communication that publishing affords, and I believe that an important part of what I do is to re-educate the perception that psychics have all the answers. Some of the people I help are vulnerable, and it is important to tread carefully with predictions in particular, because of the hope people invest in outcomes. I have come across some difficult scenarios where skills in counselling are crucial to giving someone the best chance. It is dangerous to get yourself into a situation where you are perceived as some sort of definitive oracle. This is in fact why I prefer to give my readings a spiritual angle, and place an emphasis on healing, rather than get someone hooked on the idea that their lives will be okay, only when such and such happens.

Psychic insights appeal to our innate sense of curiosity, but spiritually there are more important issues at stake than knowing when our lotto numbers are coming up.

Having been brought up in a Christian environment, I was tapped into living with a spiritual awareness from an early age. My father, as well as being a trained medical doctor, is also well known in evangelical circles as a counsellor and lecturer. With this background, working as a psychic healer was actually the last thing I had on my mind! In an unexpected way this ministry, if you dare call it that, has found me. In 1982 I went up to the Scottish universities, Stirling and Edinburgh, from my home in Bristol. Immediately I felt rather abandoned. What had I done to deserve this exile? However, several years down the line the philosophy, religious studies and publishing degrees suddenly make sense, with the rather bizarre twist of healing thrown in for good measure.

Working as a healer was not contrived or planned, rather it unfolded as I followed my instincts. I had always noticed that people who would not typically give me much attention tended to queue up when something was wrong.

Boyfriends have commented on my healing touch –but we will not pursue that line of inquiry. I remember when my father lost his sight completely for a stretch of time the different reactions of his kids were telling. My brother's response was to run to the woodshed in a bid to become MR DIY; my sister read endless stories; but I was stumped. I could only reach out with the reassurance of touch, and keep quiet when the understandable questions of "why God why?" rang around the room.

Sometimes there are no appropriate words. Things happen which seem unfair, even downright outrageous. I noticed a profound empathy for such situations, but I had not expected to become a healer. Although I was aware of the "laying on of hands" in church, I had not particularly related this gift to myself. I identify strongly with Eileen Drewery's sentiment "Why Me?" and I would recommend this book by Glen Hoddle's side kick to anyone who is interested in understanding the dynamics of healing. It is crucial for a healer not to get hooked-up on some sense of personal power. It is God who heals through the willing channel of the healer, and fairly frequently through your local GP I might add.

So how did it happen? It was only when my own life disintegrated from every angle possible that I had a profound experience of integration: all the events of my life, traumas, difficulties etc, suddenly made sense! At the time I was doing some healing on my longhaired dachshund Freddie, with another healer called Ger. The dog had been knocked over in a bizarre accident, which psychically felt like a set up. Without boring you with all the details, this proved to be a watershed in my life. The presence of Christ was strong, and I felt the somewhat contradictory strands of my life come together. I certainly went through the most brutal apprenticeship a healer could hope for.

So, is there such a thing as a tarot card reading Christian? Apparently there was for a time; although I would prefer to call myself a Christian Hermeticist. I tend not to use Tarot now with my work. But, before the clergy start praying for me, although I would be grateful if they *did*, I have done a huge amount of soul searching on this subject. I do not want to turn people on to Tarot cards – quite the opposite – but in the Vatican there are huge stained glass windows of the main trump cards. These are powerful symbols that connect with our unconscious. They are universally accessible, but since the church quite rightly frowns upon idolatry they have a mixed reputation. At the time of the inquisition people like me were slaughtered by the church. The prospect of spiritual power outside the remits of the male hierarchy generally scares people. Some of this is justified as structures are important but most of it derives from ignorance. Just as a psychic can be operating without an ounce of compassion, leaving a trail of disaster, so can a priest be self-serving and corrupt. Just as a priest can be genuine and concerned, so can a psychic of integrity provide a service that brings peace and reassurance – God moves in mysterious ways!

In my research into the world of psychic guidance, and here the clergy can breathe a sigh of relief, I have come to the conclusion that absolutely nothing replaces the value of a moment to moment trust in the Almighty. Whatever our perception of God might be, we are as well to surrender our lives to faith, trusting that there is a reason for everything. We might contrive many elaborate designs for our lives, but if they do not fit with the will of God we might as well throw in the towel before we even get started.

John Drane, one of my lecturers at Stirling university, has written an important book: *"What is the New Age still saying to the Church."* Although it is a comprehensive look at aspects of the New Age movement in my view it does not go far enough. I justified my own research into this revival of ancient spirituality as a means of getting to the bottom of things. I decided to play devil's advocate, and got directly involved with aspects of the New Age that grabbed my curiosity. I knew the investigation I was undertaking was walking a spiritual tightrope, but I decided to see where it would lead. My intention was to publish this experience, but main result of going undercover since 1986, is that I can now work with authority from the inside out. This might seem rather perverse, but at least this tactic challenges people to review their spirituality, and think. There have been so many upheavals within the church that an understanding of the competition is needed. There is a melting pot of pseudo spirituality for sale, and I would be the last person to advise someone to rush out and buy a pack of Tarot cards: I have seen the damage that they can do in the wrong hands. Foster an interest in the angelic realm by all means, but it is dangerous to rely on a pack of cards if there is misguided psychic behind them.

In the Bible there are plenty of warnings against false prophecy. Jeremiah tells us to watch out for people who "speak visions from their own minds," and John commands us to "test the spirits to see whether they are from God." There is no doubt that some people are gifted with profound imagination, and the ability to receive messages from what Carl Jung called the Collective Unconscious. But, how can we be sure what they are tapping into? It is important to take a message on board, but also to reserve judgement. Something claiming to be prophetic may be a lie designed to mislead you. Do not forget there are mischievous spirits that try to have fun at our expense! In Corinthians, Paul names prophecy as one of the most desirable gifts of the spirit. Whole-heartedly I agree. In the right context prophecy can be healing, encouraging, and positive. With wisdom and discernment there is a place for giving people hope.

It is important to be aware that there can be a huge gap between psychic ability and true spirituality. They do not necessarily travel hand in hand. Psychics are trained to think symbolically. They understand the impact that society's universally accepted images have upon our psyche. Jung called these the Archetypes of the Collective Unconscious. He believed that the process of psychic integration involved the identification and release of these ancient symbols. Jung was controversial in his time. He acknowledged the power of the mind, and accepted the existence of psychic ability. His principle of synchronicity demonstrated the phenomenon of simultaneous events and the possibility of what he called "meaningful coincidence". Jung is the reason that academics will entertain the notion of 'intuition', but extend the argument further to include "psychic occurrences" and you wander into subversive territory. This is the challenge of the PhD I was researching at UCD, and was another reason for my foray into the psychic world. I believe it is possible to present this material academically, and Carl Jung is my inspiration. I think any attempt to discredit such research stems from ignorance, and reflects the limited thinking I discussed at the beginning of this piece. Further into the future our minds will be more evolved, and we will be much more receptive to perceiving the different realms of existence. Yes, that is a prediction!

The Jewish tradition of the Kabbalah equates true wisdom with the ability to foretell the future. This is a flattering prospect for a psychic, but as I have learned there is no possibility for complacency in this profession. The challenges keep coming. Every consultation is different just as every healing session has a life of its own. This is work where guidance and intuition are strongly in play. It is not possible to pre-plan or contrive the outcome of a consultation – cynics take note! What happens is meant to happen, and I have a strong belief that the right people ask for help. Sometimes there are situations that seem to be set-up by the pranksters of the spirit world. This hazard of the trade is the reason I pray like a mad woman when I am healing someone. I do not mean to be alarmist but prayer is important because the need for protection is high. I strongly believe there is a reason for everything, challenges et al. It is important to keep perspective, and to look after yourself as a healer. At the height of the time when I saw people face to face, there were days when I delayed appointments for the sake of the client because my own energies were not right. I refused to work when I was overtired or off-colour as this was not fair on the client, and it was not fair on me. There were days when someone could offer me a ridiculous fee for a reading, and I would decline. This would probably be the most bizarre aspect of my work from the cynics point of view, but I know many healers who would support what I am saying. Healing must be performed in the right conditions, and so must psychic readings. It is actually draining to have people pulling at you for attention, especially when you are sensitive at the best of times. So it is in everyone's interest that I pace myself and do not get burned out. This is by way of apology to those still waiting.

A final thought for those still nervous about how working as a psychic connects with faith in God. As I have tried to show it is possible to look into the energies that are shaping our future, but it is not always wise to do so. True spirituality reveres simplicity, and it is good to develop contentment with the present moment of our everyday lives. Grace is certainly the most powerful energy we can ally ourselves to.

The Reluctant Psychic ~

An autobiographical note by Sarah Delamere Hurding. Psychic Researcher and Spiritual Healer.

I was born to a doctor and nurse (Roger and Joy) in Chelmsford, Essex. At the age of 6 the family moved to Bristol where I was educated. I went to Gordano Comprehensive School in Portishead, and studied mainly arts subjects.

I was going to do English at Cambridge University, but in the end decided to head for Scotland: I Studied English, Philosophy and Religious Studies at Stirling University, between 1982 and 1986.

I then worked as a chef in a German restaurant in Edinburgh. I got increasingly involved in the music business. I worked driving security on Waterboys Highlands and Islands Tour in 1990, and subsequently their support band Wee Free Kings. I spotted The Proclaimers, for the manager of the German restaurant Kenny Mac Donald, and he proceeded to manage the duo to great effect.

Eventually I set up my own company, Quantum Leap, and booked gigs for many of the Scottish bands of the early 90's: The Crows; Kith and Kin; Swamptrash; Wee Free Kings. I did a lot of touring with the American Cajun band fronted by Pierre Le Rue, formerly linked to Queen Ida, in Europe and the UK. In the middle of all this I completed my postgraduate English degree at Edinburgh University, graduating in 1988.

In March 1994 I moved to Dublin, and completed M. Phil in Publishing studies at Stirling University from my new Dublin home. Upon my arrival in Dublin I worked at U2's nightclub the Kitchen as hostess, until it's closure in April 2002. This provided hours of fun and entertainment, and much interesting gossip, some of which is depicted in my memoir Mermaid in The Kitchen.

Part of the work that I do is in the media, and I feel that increasing public awareness of all things psychic is part of my calling. I have enjoyed radio appearances on Gerry Ryan, Una Power, An Olivia, Galway Radio, Tom Dunne; Tony Fenton; TalkSport UK; News Talk 106; Spin Radio; and RTE's Liveline. Throughout 2000, into 2001, I made regular guest appearances on Ireland AM for their Psychic phone-in slot.

I was involved with the Irish Popstars series, and correctly predicted the full line-up of the band SIX. I was asked to read for the final 32 contestants for 10 minutes each. After this I placed six names in a sealed envelope (October 2001), months before the band was announced in January 2002. The envelope identified the Nadine factor. Although I knew Nadine Coyle would be initially chosen by the judges Louis Walsh, Lynda Martin and Bill Whelan: I also knew she would not be in the final band. The fact I also predicted Nadine's replacement Sarah Keating got people's attention. There is no way I could have "known" any of that.

I still write regularly for the Star Newspaper, The Sunday World, RTE Guide, Irish Independent Newspaper, Herald, and Cork Echo; and have had pieces published in most of the Irish papers. I really enjoy the journalistic part of my work, and I had for many years several books in rough format. These notes and blogs then inspired the compilation of my books *Sarah's Star Signs*, *Mermaid in The Kitchen*, *Star Scope*, and *Dear Sarah*. Because I am psychic I have always known that I would write and publish; and there are several more pieces in the pipeline.

My interest in the psychic world developed more fully when I moved to Scotland. I was brought up in a Christian family, and kept my heightened sensitivity rather quiet. I did not really know what The Gift was anyway. I just thought it was a natural normal thing. I began researching the subject, because I did not believe that a useful gift from God could be that bad. Such good things happened whenever I utilized either the guidance or the healing, that I had to understand the skills better, so that I could use them effectively to help people.

I try to bring compassion and empathy into my work at all times. I have learned how to be very careful with the subject, and am aware of the dangers and pitfalls. I think that as long as The Gift is used responsibly it has a place. The guidance that psychic insight brings is really profound, and I certainly found the ability to channel information a great help when it came to essay writing.

It is also handy when you can insist to a car salesman that the car you want definitely "out there," even if he knows it logically should not be made in that particular colour (it happened – I had that car organized by 4.30pm the same day!). My sister always remembers how I spotted her husband. She visited me in Scotland with her boyfriend and another couple, and I told her she would marry the other guy. She said "nah he's married to her." Say no more; they were married within three years.

So, being psychic provides useful hints for my nearest and dearest. But nothing beats working professionally. It is rewarding to see people who have been struggling walk out the door with a spring in their step. A good bit of counselling is involved, and usually sessions are far removed from fortune-telling. Of course the fun element has its place, which is why I enjoy the media aspect of this work.

On a more serious note I have helped the Garde and Police with certain missing person and murder cases. This work is very draining so it is only possible to be highly selective. It is really important for me to be careful of who I try to help. I can be highly unavailable to some people, and very easy to find for others. This might sound cruel, but it is the only way to function effectively, and do quality work. Long distance healing is a useful tool for those who do not get through to see me. Indeed most of my work now is done without me meeting people in person. Working with energies can be dangerous so it is important for me to monitor all these factors. Everything is energy so it is quite possible to both help and heal from a distance. In fact you should be wary of the psychic who says they *have* to meet you to help you!

Everything is energy. Therefore, I can help you wherever you are in the world.

AURA SOMA

Aura Soma is a fascinating healing system based on the mysterious contents of 100 multi-coloured bottles. The exact ingredients are kept secret, but each bottle contains a potion comprising of various herbs, crystals and colour.

Most of the combinations are two-tone and when presented together they form a beautiful display. The colours range from intense purples, blues, magentas, reds and oranges, to delicate pastels and hints of hue. Some of the layers are transparent or clear, which in Aura Soma signifies the full rainbow spectrum rather than an absence of colour. In fact, the paler the tint the more impressive the spiritual impact of the bottle. The lighter bottles connect with the energies of spiritual leaders and masters like Christ, St. Germain, and Djwhal Khul.

It was Vicky Wall who developed Aura Soma in 1984. She was a sensitive lady who always had clairvoyant awareness and healing ability. This manifested in a highly developed auric sight – she could discern a person's character in all its glory by the colours visible in their magnetic field, or aura. Vicky was a trained pharmacist who inherited her father's ability to concoct healing creams and phials of unidentified liquid. Her Hasidic Jewish upbringing gave her a legacy of intuitive discernment that she turned to good effect. With Aura Soma she has brought many non-specific and intangible issues into a physical form. A lot of the more inaccessible aspects of spirituality have been grounded in a beautiful array of colour.

The bottles represent a form of vibrational healing which works in a very subtle way on the energy systems of the body. The variety of names given to this mix of oil and water, give clues as to their possible impact. The Humpty Dumpty bottle is wonderfully restorative after shock; the Florence Nightingale soothes the convalescent, and is supportive of those with ME; the Get Up and Go gives an energy rush; and the Unconditional Love bottle helps with self-acceptance issues, and feelings pertaining to a lack of love. There are many quaintly named bottles, like Charity, Kindness, Love and Light; but there are others with real guts like Physical Rescue, I Am, and Living in the Material World.

The bottles may be applied to the body or kept in the owner's personal space - either way they work on the level they are chosen for. The applications of each bottle are many and varied, and it is best if they are selected intuitively. The bottle to take home is quite literally the bottle you would not like to leave.

In an Aura Soma reading the client selects four bottles by instinct. The first bottle describes your soul purpose on the earth at this time: the upper part reflects your circumstances and upbringing, and gives an accurate description of your personality. The lower fraction gives an indication of your life's task and reveals your true aura or colour ray.

In combination, the two layers display the nature of your soul – fairly frequently the first bottle is a persistent favourite. When this happens you can be sure you are receiving a true description of your life's path. This bottle must be considered in all of its applications: Spiritual, Mental, Emotional, and Physical.

For example, if someone always chose Maid Marion in first place they would likely be intuitive and energetic, possessing great powers of discernment and wisdom. In a negative respect they might have a tendency to be rather passive and could readily fall into playing the martyr in relationships.

Spiritually this bottle offers a refreshment course: a chance to see things from a new perspective and it would certainly help someone to break free from negative emotional entanglements. It is very supportive to females experiencing divorce and separation.

The second choice in a reading reveals where a person's difficulties and challenges lie. It can often indicate the past struggles which have brought them to where they are today. The second bottle displays the gift of negative experiences, and ultimately shows how these can be turned to good effect. If someone chose Wings of Healing in second place it would indicate that they have felt misunderstood and rejected, and may have reacted with suicidal thoughts. The gift in this situation, is that the isolated person has huge potential for empathy, and possible healing abilities.

Ultimately, such a process can strengthen a person to the point where they are formidable: aware of their life purpose and at one with themselves and God.

The third bottle reveals the present situation, and indicates how far along the path the client has travelled. It is important to take note of the negative personality traits at this point, as these show the stumbling blocks to future development.

The green/magenta combination in third place (named The Wanderer) would demonstrate possessiveness and negative behavioural patterns in relationships. If such a problem is not addressed, the person stands to repeat the cycles of relating that have marred his or her relationships to date. Feelings of jealousy and envy must be resolved, or this person will remain emotionally stunted and restricted.

The choice of bottles thus far gives a detailed picture of someone's life to date. For this reason people can find an Aura Soma reading a surprisingly moving experience. It is often disconcerting how a row of four - admittedly beautiful – bottles can reveal so much. Indeed, we are only scratching the surface of what the bottles are capable of. They also have connections with the Kabbalah, the Tarot cards, and the I-Ching. Each bottle may be interpreted intuitively by an experienced reader, and if that were not enough, they often take on individual formations and colours (I have seen mermaids, dolphins, and figures formed in the oils of the top fraction).

Finally, the fourth bottle speaks of the future, and indicates the form this might take if the person remains in their particular groove. This is a dynamic choice as we have the free will to reshape our future by working on the issues at hand (as revealed by the reading). It is beneficial to place the fourth bottle by the bed. This invites the positive energies of the future in, and means the bottle is working in advance to set up the appropriate conditions for our best development.

The reading at this level is mainly spiritual, however the bottles do have physical applications which may be addressed as the need arises. For example, A Chain of Flowers (no. 11) supports a woman who is trying to conceive a child, and although there are no guarantees, the bottle gives the woman the best chance in this respect. There are also wonderful skin creams amongst the range of bottles (those with pale magenta in particular), and the Peace bottle is very good for stretch marks!

The Aura Soma collection is at the very least an aesthetically pleasing array of colour. It should be explored on the level that feels comfortable or which makes sense. As I have illustrated it goes very deep – but you have to want it to, (there are no rules).

Most people can accept the attraction of the bottles, and Vicky herself always noticed with amusement how the stressed out businessmen consistently chose the blue/blue Peace bottle from her stand. As with most things spiritual Aura Soma meets us at a place we understand, and if that constitutes a challenge, so be it.

CHAPTER ONE:
Psychic Ability –The Gift

Subject: **Can I Learn To Be Psychic?**

Aura Soma Bottle # 33 (Dolphin- Royal Blue/Turquoise) helps the development of Clairvoyant ability if there is intrinsic talent.

Dear Sarah
Is it possible to learn to be psychic? I have had lots of readings. But I want to set up my own business doing readings. No one in my family had The Gift. How do set things up?

There is no easy answer to the "how psychic am I?" question. We are all born with a degree of intuition that may indeed be developed. And all of us have an in built awareness that we should trust our instincts when push comes to shove. Problems arise however, when the whole world and his auntie suddenly set up shop! I often compare psychic ability to artistry: We can all paint some kind of picture, but not all of us are budding Picasso's. Hence the label "The gift" is attributed to those who genuinely "see" visions or get messages.

In the deep distant past there was a sense of reverence and mystery given to those with second sight. Spooky, the witches in Macbeth may be, but they *had* something! Nowadays psychics, mindbenders, healers and mediums are crawling out of every nook and cranny. There is an astrological reason for this. The Age of Aquarius heightens our senses for all things spiritual. Many people are waking up to the Sixth Sense, and are seeking to develop it. It may begin as a vague interest or fanatical hobby. But then develop into either a genuine ability to help people, or a load of old nonsense. This leads me to the other question of motivation and integrity. Many times psychic friends of mine have had to pick up the pieces for people who have been left distraught and misled by readings.

The seriousness of this responsibility is not funny. When people trust you for guidance and snippets of the future you have to deliver or retire! I have seen so much damage done by readers who present information in a definite way. Then the exact opposite happens, and the person concerned is left deceived and reeling. So be careful out there. To be honest, I would love to see Hogwart's become a reality. But, unless you have inherited a family "Gift" that has been tried and tested down the aeons, it would be advisable to take it easy – certainly do not run before you can walk. Also, I would stress that working spiritually and psychically is very much a vocation or a calling. It cannot be contrived. Plenty of people *do* set themselves up for financial gain. But you will find that this motivation backfires in the long run. How many millionaire psychics do you know? This takes me back to days gone by again, when the psychic or gypsy would read in return for food, bedding or clothing! Without meaning to be blasphemous, the calling to work spiritually is just that: a calling. It is not done for personal gain. It is done because you feel compelled to heal and help people.

If you are going into this esoteric and mystical work professionally, you can expect strange things to happen which will continually challenge your choice of vocation. Some of the tests are funny – be warned! There should in fact be "danger money" when you are doing this properly. Healers not properly protected with the correct techniques have been known to take on the ailments of their clients for example. Sometimes the price to pay is literally too high.

Skills in counselling are always useful, and an awareness of energy is absolutely fundamental. I have seen people come unstuck big time because they listened to misguided readers with good intentions.

It is a minefield out there, and the more sophisticated you become the more sneaky the traps get; and the more testing the challenges. Lessons of trust are a given, and none of this should be done lightly. This is not an easy meal ticket, as many would have you believe. Quite the opposite. Mystics pay a high price to "walk the path."

Both *Harry Potter*, and *The Lord of the Rings*, give an excellent portrayal of what you are up against doing this work for the "Light." Look at the power of "The Ring," and do not get seduced by it. The more Harrys Gandalfs we have at large the better. Just make sure you get a measure of what is involved. Once you embark, the rest will unfold; and everyone's road is completely different. I can only give you the warnings, rather than the details.

Subject: **World Trade Centre 9:11**

Aura Soma Bottle # 26 (Humpty Dumpty- Orange/Orange) for shock. Bottle # 94 (Archangel Michael- Pale Blue/Pale Yellow) to resonate with the energy of the Tower with high protection from disturbance.

Dear Sarah
We are all panicking about my step-uncle. He was due on the 105th floor of the second tower in New York yesterday. The rest of the family is fine. They live 20 mins from the World Trade centre. They are huddled around the TV, dust everywhere. What is going to happen to us all? Was this disaster foreseen?

Do not worry about your uncle. I think you know deep down that he is okay. Actually by the time I write this he will have been home a week. He got caught up helping people and accompanied a woman to hospital. You mentioned the phone call in your letter – I expect that was him trying to get through from the streets nearby.

This terrible atrocity was foreseen in different ways, but sometimes the feelings that accompany such visions are so awful you don't want to dwell on them. Since Bush came to power in the States a lot of us have been feeling uncomfortable. It was inevitable that he would take the first opportunity to display America's might; and amidst the aftermath of this carnage he will do so.

Words cannot express the despicable nature of what these "terrorists" have done. The way the West responds to this is the greatest challenge ever put to humanity. Thank God we have taken the time to pray, mourn and grieve. The blessing in this darkness is that we are turning to God. Our spirituality is "on call." This is a time for compassion and understanding. In my view a measured response is much smarter than aggression. The opportunity for massive destruction has never been higher. Action engages us all in a war that will take no prisoners.

The West should now review its policies, rebuild its economy, and make damn sure they get the right men for this. Unfortunately, both Blair and Bush are thinking big. In principle this is correct, but the reality will not be pretty. This attack on New York was humbling and shocking in the extreme. But if great care is not taken what follows could be worse.

What disturbs me psychically about this is the way that Bin Laden is being hounded. Do not get me wrong, he is no angel, but the man behind these attacks is Hussein. Well, he will be the fall guy; put it like that. This act of war is a taunt to the West that goes back to the Gulf War. It has been meticulously planned since then. It is Hussein's masterminded attempt to revenge the way we flattened Iraq. I knew this as soon as I saw the planes go into the towers. Look at who was in power – another Bush! Okay, Bin Laden was not complaining, but he was an agreed scapegoat of both East and West. This distraction means those intent on serious invasion can get on with their work. What is disturbing is that there are units like this all over Europe and America. The infiltration of the West is massive.

This is indeed an opportune time to root out the evil of terrorism. But as we all know the possibility of hypocrisy is immense. We should all look carefully to ourselves, rather than get carried away on a tide of retribution and revenge.

Subject: **Clairvoyant 'Gift'**

Aura Soma Bottle # 33 (Dolphin- Royal Blue/Turquoise) assists someone whom is truly clairvoyant.

Dear Sarah
Have I lost my psychic gift? I was given the gift 10 years ago. I came out into the open with it and endured a lot of suffering because of people's attitude to it. My health suffered especially when I discovered I could see into the spirit world. I let it go. Stopped foretelling the future. Was I wrong to do this? Does it prove I was not a good candidate for the gift? I long to have been a proper psychic.

In a way you are right to have stepped back from working as a psychic. When you see the suffering it brought to your family, it was a sensible thing to do. It is not an easy road at the best of times; and being aware of energies and symbolic messages is guaranteed to make a normal life impossible. You have to be very balanced and objective to handle visions and pictures. It is possibly not an accident that psychic is next to psycho in the dictionary! I am only kidding; but you have first-hand experience of what I am talking about. I have heard of people praying to have clairvoyant sight taken away because they believe it to be sinful. I do not believe it is. It is in fact one of the Gifts of The Spirit mentioned in The Bible; so long as the source of your information is The Holy Spirit, of course.

In the wrong hands psychic information can cause chaos. It can indeed be sinful if it takes you down a track that leads away from faith in the almighty. Potentially it can mess with your perception of reality and consequently your choices. Really it is better not to work psychically if you are at all uneasy. There are many occupational hazards that are unseen and treacherous. You have to be sure that you are tapping into the right stuff, otherwise in all honesty you are setting yourself up for a fall.

As you found out it can be a thankless occupation at times. People can expect you to perform, sort out their problems, and accurately guarantee them a rosy future.. Quite a task and of course it brings a huge responsibility with it. Only you can make these decisions and judgements for yourself. Why not pray for angelic guidance and support?

The Bible is full of vision and prophecy, so predictive work is not inherently wrong. The gift is meant to encourage, heal and help people. Really, how can that be wrong? But remember the road to hell is paved with good intentions. You are playing with spiritual fire if you take away the right we all have to make our own choices. Nothing is set in stone, but we do all have a destiny to fulfil. Sometimes silence is golden; and it is better not to predict than to predict inaccurately. We do not have to know our future. The present is usually more than ok if only we would open our eyes and appreciate it.

Having said that people need counsel and good advice, so it is better to work with your gift if it genuinely helps people. The important thing is to constantly review your motives and integrity. If you have any doubts disconnect as much as you can. Having said that, it is not an easy ride to dismount from. Some say it is impossible, once you are underway.

Subject: **Can I Switch off My Psychic Ability?**

Aura Soma Bottle # 35 (Kindness- Pink/Violet) will assist you in healing others and yourself.

Dear Sarah
I am a bit psychic and very sensitive to things around me. Lately it has been getting overpowering, could you tell me how to switch this off when I want to? What is my future in relation to healing and being psychic? I really need to know how to switch off to this.

Being psychic is a gift and nothing to panic about. Really it is best to remain down to earth and grounded. You do not have to walk around in a permanent state of psychic arousal! It is perfectly okay to get on with a normal life and not use The Gift, except when you choose. Just because you are a little sensitive does not mean that you have to run out and save the world. Sometimes it is best to function within the sphere of your personal environment and help only those close to you.

Being sensitive and a little paranoid does not a psychic make. There are some people who believe they are more psychic than they actually are. These people are dangerous to themselves and others. It is a huge responsibility using such gifts to help those who ask, so if you have doubts just switch off. You can decide to do this for yourself. Or if you find that you are really troubled, a priest may help you close-down your channels. You may pray to have your visions and pictures taken away. It all depends where your messages are coming from.

But why block the good stuff when it can help, heal and guide? If you find that you are disturbed persistently by negative thoughts and superstitious compulsions it would be wise to seek help. But do not be afraid. Fear feeds itself, and doubts, worries and confusion only add to the chaos.

The best way forward is to trust yourself, and your own spiritual development. Work more closely with the angels. Ask for their guidance and protection.

You can pray that if this way of being is not right for you, it may be taken away. On the other hand, if you are here to serve and help others, pray for clarity.

God helps those who help themselves, so be sensible. Do not lose the run of yourself with all things psychic. It is a gift we all have in some measure, but we make mistakes when we give into it completely. Some objectivity is needed in order to test the messages we are given. But if we live only by logic, we miss much of the mystery and beauty of life.

Working with angels will develop your appreciation of synchronicity. There is no need to cut the magic out of life. Just make sure that you replace fear with wonder.

There is no point in curling up in a corner, when you can be out in the world shining bright.

Subject: Developing The Gift

Aura Soma Bottle # 78 (Crown Rescue- Violet/Deep Magenta) helps to open the third eye. Bottle # 33 (Dolphin- Royal Blue/Turquoise). Bottle # 24 (New Message: Soul Mate- Violet/Turquoise) are bottles that support psychic work.

Dear Sarah
I am constantly being told that I am psychic by healers and psychics. I have Tarot cards and have had a bit of success. I wonder could you tell me if I am psychic and how to develop it.

My first impression from the energy of your letter is that you do have healing ability. However I also wonder why you are running around to different people looking for validation. It is rarely useful to visit all possible psychics in the hope that they will manifest a life for you. This approach can actually be quite undermining of your personal power.

We are the co-creators of our lives and expecting readers to produce the magic formula for a wonderful future is a form of laziness. People have a tendency to elevate and mystify psychic gifts. They can be developed and we all have a taste of them in some measure. However, it is very self-defeating if not self-destructive to put your life into the hands of a stranger. The psychic you mention in your letter has a reputation of telling people much the same thing in readings. She is essentially a performer who has her act down to a tee. Sadly some people take advantage of their status and client list and make a fortune. By all means go along for the entertainment value, but do remember she has just told the person two in front the same thing.

Having said that if you choose to put a value upon a particular reading that is fine. Even the worst readers hit the nail on the head with some things. The danger is going in blind and forgetting that sometimes a little knowledge is worse than none at all. Be wise and only accept what makes sense to you. The potential for the sabotage of your life is immense if you continue to look for reassurance in this way.

In your case I would recommend that you sit quiet and ask yourself a few questions. We all have the answers to life's dilemmas deep within our psyche. So the best way to develop the ability to receive messages is to listen to your own heart and soul. Work with your own guides and angels. Do not put your trust in psychics who may not be working with the clearest energies and information.

To be a clear channel you need to look after yourself, to protect your space and to meditate. It can be as basic as a healthy diet, a walk on the beach and a reverent approach to life. God holds the key to all the guidance we need. There is no need to make your life even more complicated by listening to many interpretations and predictions.

Simplicity is the key to clarity. The best psychic information has a practical and tangible application. It does not remain up there in the clouds. It brings messages we can work with and apply to our lives. I do not see the point of readings that feed you your dreams on a plate and then leave you dangling. That is unfair and corrupt and it helps no one. In fact more often than not it actually prevents you from getting on with your life because you are too busy waiting for the stuff that is supposed to happen. Such readings cause confusion, unhappiness and frustration. Working with God and your angels does not.

Subject: **Will I Win The Lottery?**

Aura Soma Bottle # 19 (Living in the Material World- Red/Purple) supports finances. Bottle # 79 (Ostrich- Orange/Violet) will help the spiritual shock and deception.

Dear Sarah
A psychic told me last year that I would definitely win the lottery very soon. I trusted what he said and took out a loan to keep me going in the meantime. Recently I challenged him about this and he said the win is on its way but that I should not have counted on it. How do I get out of this mess?

If we were living in Atlantean times you would be able to sue this man for spiritual deception. It is inexcusable that someone should have commandeered your life in this way. To be told in such definite terms that you would win money has left you vulnerable and desperate. In fact you have made decisions that you would not normally have made. Psychics have a huge responsibility in the way they present messages to people, and here is one example of how things can go wrong.

If I could have 100 Euro for everyone who has been told that they will win money by a psychic I would be a rich woman. Do not get me wrong, people *do* win huge amounts of money when it is their destiny to do so. But the problems arise if we assume this destiny for ourselves when it is not really in our control, nor is it our decision. Never bank upon a win of money before it materializes.

The good news is the information you were given may actually turn out to be correct. But in the here and now you have a practical problem to clear up.

There is a mixed blessing in knowing the future. For there is a danger we may take inappropriate action before the foreseen event. It is a mistake to believe that such an event is just around the corner. Divine timing is completely different to our linear sense of time. Just because you are told something will happen do not act as if it already has. We have to live within the constrictions of time and space on the earth plane.

It is not advisable to take the messages from the astral level and trust them completely. You have displayed innocence, and trusted privileged information. Do not be dismayed, as the universe will honour your integrity. What you have done has defied all the laws of logic but it is when you step out in faith that miracles happen.

If you take on board the subtle spiritual lessons of this situation, you will realise that it is wrong to put your life into someone else's hands. The answers to your problems lie deep within your soul. On a practical level you can make the money to repay any debt. What is more important is that you become the master of your own destiny. Access your inner *deserving* of this win, and it will land for you. Trust yourself in the future and pray for guidance. The universe has enough for everyone, so do not panic about the bills. If you spend fearlessly the energy of money is such that it will return effortlessly to you. It is poverty consciousness that restricts you and actually blocks the win of money. Surrender the issue and if it is meant to be, the jackpot will be yours minus this trauma.

Subject: **Whom To Trust?**

Aura Soma Bottle # 79 (Ostrich Bottle- Orange/Violet) releases the individual from spiritual shock and helps assimilate the lessons. Bottle # 25 (Florence Nightingale- Purple/Magenta) helps to liberate you from disappointment.

Dear Sarah
I have gone to a lot of so-called fortune-tellers in the Mid-West, and I have been told such nonsense. Can you advise me on whom or what to trust – I need to know if I will find happiness? Do you have any spiritual advice?

In response to the issues you raise about fortune-tellers I would urge you to be careful. There are a few good psychics in Ireland and dozens of mediocre ones. On the world stage, you could say there are hundreds and thousands of "okay" psychics and mediums "out there." But still only a handful of absolutely brilliant ones.

Please keep an open mind if you go for a reading. It is dangerous to rely too heavily upon what a fortune-teller might say. The reality is that in the wrong hands the Tarot cards can cause a lot of heartache, disillusionment and disappointment. Mischievous energies are prevalent in the spirit world, and to put it bluntly they can have fun with us. It takes a skilled psychic – who is a pure and accurate channel – to give a reading that is trustworthy.

This is work that carries a huge responsibility and should not be treated lightly. There is a tendency to deceive ourselves that it is all a bit of fun. It does have curiosity value certainly, but psychic work attracts a lot of vulnerable people. If you are desperate and are being sold inaccurate information it serves to twist your mind further. There is no doubt that belief in a dream can keep us going on one level, but ultimately it is not useful to hold onto things that have no bearing on reality.

Do not get me wrong, good psychics *can* predict the future but it is very important not to get obsessed by the timing of positive events - most psychics are notoriously bad at timing!

Spiritual energies do not have the same notion of time as we do – a lifetime passes in the blink of an eye. Psychic readings step outside of time, and it is difficult to assess when an event will ground itself. They tune into snippets of our past, present and future, and often the messages are symbolic rather than factual - discernment is crucial for effective interpretation.

We all have a tendency to elevate psychic ability because of its mystery. It holds a fascination that grabs our imagination. It is important to remember that psychics are human and mistakes are made.

When our lives are in turmoil two things happen: we review the past and we hope for a better future. We can become a 'record' replaying the scenarios we believe went wrong, or we can hold fast to a future where all our dreams come true. Either way we are losing the joy of life in the present. A responsible psychic will ensure that you have the ability to engage in the here and now.

Some hope for the future is of course important, but it is best not to completely rob life of its mystery. Always trust your own instincts – use outside guidance if you need to, but hold onto a healthy scepticism. There are many paths to our destiny and the main thing of importance is to take responsibility for your own future. Fate does not write everything in stone; we have freedom of will to play with.

Subject: **Misleading Information**

Aura Soma Bottle # 50 (El Morya- Pale Blue/Pale Blue) puts you in touch with Divine will. Bottle # 79 (Ostrich- Orange/Violet) will help you overcome spiritual deception.

Dear Sarah
I feel let down by the predictions of a spiritualist friend. I'm quite angry with her as I feel I would not be in the situation I'm now in. I'm 22 with a three months old son. Will I find happiness and unconditional love?

My first impression on reading your letter is that you are coping with a lot at a young age. I think you are mildly depressed, so perhaps seek help for this if it does not improve in the next month or so. You also should take responsibility for your choices. Your spiritualist friend means well, but a little knowledge is dangerous.

Information is not automatically validated just because it is psychic. It is important to test the messages and retain some objectivity. Do not assume that every psychic offers profound advice. Only time will tell the significance of a reading, but it is important to assume responsibility for what you choose to believe.

You would strongly benefit from healing as the father of your child has put you through the mill. He is young and immature and lashes out in anger at the predicament he finds himself in. Again he is not accepting responsibility. He will not change in a hurry, and I do not think you can expect much from him at this stage. Please do not put on a brave face just for the sake of it. You need support, so be honest when you are not coping. Your friends and family will help.

It is important not to punish yourself. Life has not deliberately dealt you a bad hand. You were destined to have this child and as you admit, you love him to bits. So allow him to be the joy in your life at this point. Realise that his father has a lot of growing up to do, and leave him to it.

You are a survivor, and although you had big hopes you can modify them. There is something to be said for getting realistic. It is a shame that this has cramped your style, but you will find happiness if you embrace the situation.

Do not expect unconditional love from anybody. Humans are not the best at this. We all tend to project conditions and expectations onto our relationships. It is only God and dogs who love unconditionally. Having said that, you will have a very fulfilling and romantic marriage. There is certainly a very happy family situation developing over the next three years, and I believe you will have a daughter by choice. You do not have to carry a sense of being stuck. Hold onto the positive love you have for your son, and trust that the right partner will appear at the right time. Because he will!

Subject: **Mediumship**

Aura Soma Bottle # 65 (Head in Heaven & Feet on Earth- Violet/Red) helps clairvoyance. Bottle #19 (Living in the Material World- Red/Violet) protects from mischievous entities.

Dear Sarah

I am writing to you about my future. Sometimes I get so down and out no matter how hard I try things go drastically wrong. My mother is a psychic and medium and has great belief in me. I feel she is just saying that and is keeping things from me.

I am a little concerned at the energies that surround you. I hope that your mother's work has not made you over sensitive to things spiritual. You sound depressed in your letter, and it feels as if you are under a cloud. I presume that your mother understands the importance of protection.

It is very dangerous to get complacent when dabbling with the spirit world. Really, it is better not to do it at all. Sometimes our curiosity for knowledge takes us to places that are less than wholesome.

Nothing beats prayer when we are searching for answers to the things that trouble us. I have said this before, but is possible to be fed false information by mischievous entities. The Bible recommends strongly that we "test the spirits." I do not feel it is a particularly good sign that you are so oppressed and cannot fully understand why.

I am sure that your mother means well and encourages you wholeheartedly. But you need to cleanse both your environment and your spirit. I do not mean this in a preachy way, but you must address the energies of your home in particular.

There are some wonderful products made by Aura Soma that can protect you, and transform negative or stagnant vibrations. The Arch-Angel Michael bottle is very powerful, as is the St. Germain Quintessence. Serapis Bey is like spiritual disinfectant and there are bottles to support effective mediumship.

As I have implied this work is not to be taken lightly. People can get caught with the assumption that The Gift gives them free reign with the lives of others. Sometimes it is more responsible to keep quiet.

A break from the intensity of such work is crucial. Real life can be both a tonic and an antidote. Switching off spiritually can be as important to our equilibrium as getting tuned-in. You must learn to discern which is needed. At this point in your life, if I could send you to American boot camp I would!

My point is, of course you will be fine but perhaps at the moment this "awareness" is not in your best interests. Sometimes, for the purposes of grounding, and common sense utilization, it is best to just "be." Relax and do the next thing. Your Gifts will naturally find their path at the right time. In your case I strongly do not suggest that you force their development in *any* way.

Let it be an organic part of you that comes to the fore, only when it is meant to. Naturally and effortlessly.

Subject: **Confused Readings**

Aura Soma Bottle # 54 (Serapis Bey-Clear/Clear) helps us find truth and clarity and shifts negative energy.

Dear Sarah
I have been very confused by psychic readings in the past and have received a lot of conflicting information. I want to make a go of it in the States but I'm terrified I will fail as I am in debt back home. One psychic said I would go for a few days another that I could settle over there. What is the story?

My answer to you would be in the form of a question. What do you want to happen? Decide what you want and go out there and get it!

Every time you visit a psychic you are handing your life over to someone else. Interesting and entertaining it might be to put your life in the hands of a stranger, but is it responsible? No!

I can see from your letter that you have been led a merry dance. The many different readings you have attended have left you confused and understandably bitter.

The universe does not actually like it if we over ask a question, or try to second-guess every fine detail. Trust is everything. Receive and accept the energy of a good reading, and then allow it to unfold. When you keep "picking away" at the same question, a funky thing happens; and the thing you so desire does not.

Over asking acts as a block on the very thing we wish for. So, "let go and let God."

The power of a potent accurate reading is undeniable, but this is where we may come unstuck. I do not want to alarm you but there are also mischievous energies that try to have fun at our expense. If we choose to lay ourselves open to this energetic form of ping-pong, we can expect quite devastating consequences. Psychics need to be aware of the huge responsibility they have to the general public who put themselves forward for readings.

In my opinion this is a serious business and should not be viewed as entertainment. Nor should it be seen as a way to sell people their dreams. Leading people down the garden path is spiritual deception at its worst. So be careful that you fully trust your reader and reserve judgement until you see the evidence with your own eyes.

Never make an important decision based upon a reading even if the psychic is plausible. Make sure it resonates with your own energy, as you do not have to accept blindly what you are told. This is how people get caught out, and in a way the more powerful a reader, the more potential there is for damage to be done.

Think about it! You might laugh when you exit the tent of Gypsy Lee at the local fair who tells you money is on the way. But go to a reader who is hitting the spot with everything else, and you just might get caught on the hop.

Your destiny is not written in stone, and you have more creativity at your disposal than you realise. Learn to listen to your self and trust that small whisper within which guides you through your daily life. The more you listen, the more you hear.

For a reading to make sense it must tap into your unconscious and bring forth what you already know. You can learn to do this yourself and the lesson is in the doing.

Psychic ability is something we all possess in some measure, so get busy and you will not need to rely on strangers for insight.

Subject: **Pop Star Fantasy?**

Aura Soma Bottle # 24 (New Message- Violet/Turquoise) helps you to remain open to all the new opportunities and possibilities in your life.

Dear Sarah

I am confused. I am still quite young, but was told recently by a psychic that I would be famous and even "end up" with my favourite rock star. I do not understand how this can happen. Is it true?

I do not want to be the one to dash your hopes and dreams, but you do have to keep a sense of reality. You know this which is why you are confused. Your heart is telling you one thing, and your head is telling you another. It is very common, indeed it is very much a part of growing up, to experience a crush or several. Sometimes you may hanker for the boy-next-door, other times the guy on your wall is the one you dream about. Do not necessarily put it down to your age either. There is many a housewife out there with illusions of an encounter with Brad Pitt or George Clooney.

Fantasies are an important aspect of life. There are times when they cheer us up and pull us out of the hum-drum of everyday existence. We all need dreams to focus on and wishes to hope for. Why do so many of us zoom out for the lottery tickets every Saturday!

Where things get interesting, sorry confusing, is when you move in circles where dreams merge with reality – ie) in the entertainment business. If you pursue your talents, which I believe you should, you will rub shoulders with interesting people. You need to be prepared to keep your feet on the ground and your wits about you. The film and music industries in particular are worlds rampant with egos, and full of traps you can fall into. Expect people to be out for themselves and to take advantage. Similarly to the modelling agencies that rip young girls off for dubious portfolio shots, there are those who may offer help even while leading you up the garden path. This is a world of illusion, (and damn hard work incidentally), where everything is not as it seems.

Of course there are sharks in many walks of life, but do watch out in particular, for the psychics who sell you your dreams. Your destiny is in your own hands, follow your heart by all means, but do not wear rose-tinted spectacles while you do so. My Nan once told me not to spend my life "chasing rainbows." Sure I did not really listen, but it is good advice, do you not think?

Well, that was the reality check! Now, go for gold, and follow through everything you want to achieve. Certainly never undersell yourself, and expect the best at all times. The people who succeed in this business know how to objectify themselves as a product, and most importantly, they know how to keep a semblance of privacy. The really clever ones feed lines to the media in order to throw them off track. If this is the world you want to inhabit be aware of how it all works. Having said that, of course it is the arena in which to express yourself and your creativity to good effect. You need to be sure of your motivation and integrity.

Focus on where you want to get to and do not be put off by rejection. It is a tough business to break into, but remember true talent speaks for itself and will not be missed; never mind Simon Cowell! (Having said the shows he presents are indeed an amazing way to be "spotted." Let us not be too snobby about it).

Subject: **Destiny: Can We Change It?**

Aura Soma Bottle # 50 (El Morya- Pale Blue/Pale Blue) helps us to discern Divine Will and to make appropriate, free decisions.

Dear Sarah
Is my Destiny really set in stone? Do I have to take as red everything I've been told by psychics? Can I change what is supposed to happen?

The answer to your question is "yes and no." You are raising the age-old issues that have troubled theologians and philosophers for aeons. How much freewill do we actually have? As with all things balance is the key to unlocking the best understanding of Fate and the grip it supposedly has. I almost want to ask you how much freedom do you want to exercise? There is passivity involved in attending a myriad of psychics, interesting though it may be. You are laying yourself open. Indeed you are inviting someone to tell you what is *going* to happen!

Be aware that esoteric seeds are powerful, whomever they may be planted by. In the very asking you are handing your life over to the discretion of the reader. This is all very well if you trust the person. But how can you be sure, what is really going on energetically, psychologically and spiritually? The answer is you cannot. My advice to you is that you "cannot be too careful!"

Take a tip from the male of the species for five minutes. Yes, they do possess certain pragmatic wisdom. Although I *do* help many men with guidance and healing, in general men tend *not* to enjoy handing their lives over for someone else to pass judgement on. The reason being of course? They like to think they are in control of their lives and the events thereof. Women on the other hand are ruled, well, let us say "influenced" by the moon; hormonally and otherwise. This lays them open to the famous women's intuition; and explains their susceptibility to all things psychic and spiritual.

The expression "women are from Venus and men are from Mars" applies to all life's dimensions, not just the physical.

Men would be great champions for the existence of freewill, albeit for the wrong reasons. Logical thinkers rely on the facts and figures gleaned from the metaphorical "left-side" of the human brain. Hard evidence is needed to convince those imprisoned by the limitations of their restrictive thinking. The doubting Thomas brigade have a point. Generally, macho thinkers try to control the shape of their lives in every detail. Aside from following the odd hunch, these cynics follow through only when logic dictates.

Psychic messages derive from creativity, apparently housed in the "right-side" of the brain. This aspect of the psyche is able to access the Unconscious. Artists, writers and journalists use this channel of information, often without being particularly aware of the link between creativity and psychic ability. Consequently blocks appear, as does a fear of following things through to their (logical!) conclusion.

When psychic ability is understood, mastered and respected, something *happens*. A different kind of power and control kicks in. Those who fear the unknown and perhaps their own creativity find it impossible to believe in the validity of prediction. It is not possible to predict the future, right? *Wrong!* But it begs the question is it *right* to predict the future, and to put our lives into the hands of those who can? These are complex areas that I have tackled in my memoir Mermaid in The Kitchen; so do take a look at that book if you feel so inclined. Be careful out there…

Subject: **Are Tarot Cards Evil?**

Aura Soma Bottle #24 (New Message- Violet/Turquoise) is a clairvoyant's bottle and helps you connect with a new perception of the Truth.

Dear Sarah
I want to develop my psychic abilities. What are Tarot cards and where do they come from? Do I need them? I am from a Christian home so have heard that the tarot is evil. Is this true?

Anything spiritual or psychic can be used in a good or bad way. It depends upon your motivation and integrity. If you have a simple trust and faith in God what more would you need? But even within the confines of church law there is a place for prophecy and guidance. Tarot cards are a tool that some psychics use in order to focus their energies. If you are truly psychic they are actually not necessary. It is possible to tune into people using anything you care to mention. I have been known to read toast and pints of beer.

There are signs and symbols in the strangest places if you are open and aware: from the stones on the beach, the clouds in the sky, to the coffee granules in your cup. Even the way a waiter puts down your plate can have inherent meaning. Synchronicity moments are fascinating. Now I am not recommending that you lose the plot, and start to read something into everything. But there are ways to enhance your life by being open to the different ways in which the angels and guides communicate.

To be honest it is probably best to leave the Tarot cards to the professionals. It is better to walk in tune with yourself and God than to become reliant on a deck of cards. This reflects the understandable concern that the church has with the tarot. Having said that it is often overlooked that the symbolic images of the Tarot are used in stained glass windows in the Vatican; and that Chartres cathedral in France has a round window displaying the astrology symbols. The Church has panicked throughout history over losing its patriarchal grip. This is why thousands of intuitive women were burned at the stake or dunked in water. They were probably healing and guiding in their own independent way and the church did not like it. What is your definition of evil? Murder, or trying to make a difference by helping people?

The Tarot contains images that reflect Man's path to enlightenment. They help the psychic connect with the unconscious of the person sitting in front of them. I would never encourage familiarity with the tarot as a way to get through life. In the wrong hands a lot of damage is done.

It is much better to trust yourself as all the answers we need are held deep within our own psyche. A good psychic will access this information for you; a bad one will throw you off track and even sabotage your destiny. Trust yourself. Your own guides have your best interests at heart, so listen to yourself.

The Bible challenges us to test the spirits and any information we receive. Sadly some people sell lies and the tarot does have a reputation for leading people astray. So make sure any messages you get resonate with your energy and make sense to you. The truth has quite a different feel to it than a pack of lies from a pack of cards. Their level of accuracy all depends upon who is using them.

Subject: **Is Fortune Telling Unreliable?**

Aura Soma Bottle # 72 (The Clown- Blue/Orange) Brings peace and calm after shock. It allows you to receive the kingdom of heaven like a child.

Dear Sarah
I have gone to fortune-tellers in the past, and very little of what I've been told has happened. How do I know what to trust? What is the point of readings if they are not true?

If I could count this complaint on the fingers of one hand I would not be quite so concerned. But I get many letters about readings that have caused people upset and distress.

The reason some psychics access information that turns out to be false is that they are tapping into universal thought forms.

The astral plane holds all kinds of information, some of which may be grounded, some of which may not. It is ignorance about the messages that leads to misinterpretation.

A fundamental part of working effectively as a psychic is the ability to discern the spirits. The Bible warns about this. I have mentioned it before, but there are many mischievous spirits out there who get their kicks out of our confusion.

The difference between fortune telling and prophetic vision is the difference between fast food and Caviar. Now some people hate Caviar, but it is usually those with fine taste and discernment that appreciate nourishment in a pure form.

Junk food is fine it hits the spot. But be aware that the quick fix does not offer long term sustenance. Sometimes we need to have our dreams and fantasies reinforced.

Human beings cannot cope with too much reality. But it is not really helpful to exist for too long carrying false hope. I think most of us if we are honest want to get our lives on the straight road ahead. Cul-de-sacs and blind alleys serve a purpose but they do not really get us anywhere.

So please keep an open mind if you go to a psychic reader. Always reserve judgement. It is important not to hand your power over to the point where you expect someone else to make your decisions. This can lead to a perception that trust has been betrayed if the information turns out to be wrong.

Sometimes our guides work through readers to teach us lessons. So even false information serves a purpose if it leads us to review where we place our trust.

Remember that there is no one who knows your life path as well as you.

A skilled clairvoyant, who is a pure and accurate channel may be helpful, but please do not expect them to live your life for you. This takes the mystery and surprise from life, and may lead to resentment and recriminations. At the end of the day, the person responsible for your life is *you!*

Subject: **Draining Work Situation**

Aura Soma Bottle # 6 (The Energy Bottle- Red/Red) is very energising. Similarly Bottle # 89 (Energy Rescue- Red/Deep Magenta) will help if deeper negative issues are at play.

Dear Sarah
I am working for someone highly psychic. At first I was in awe of them. Now I feel they are using their powers to keep me in my place. Going into work is now a struggle. I feel tired and low in energy. Should I leave?

There are things that you can do to protect yourself if you want to stay in your job. Why should you be manipulated against your will? Stand up to this person. The best action is to reflect any negativity straight back to them. Do not do this with any malicious intent or you will only harm yourself. Rather pray for release from this psychic attack and send any deliberate manipulation back to them with love. Such people end up hurting themselves. They believe that they can control and plot the course of their lives. They know they have power and yet do not use it altruistically. The energies of this abuse will inevitably cause them to self-combust.

They say that power corrupts and it is no more apparent than in the psychic world. We all get a kick out of someone who can read us particularly if they have never met us before. It has become a form of entertainment. Put these gifts into the hands of the ruthless, ambitious and manipulative and destruction is not far off. Remember Hitler's command of the German nation? That kind of megalomania is awesome and scary. Sometimes the best option is to run and hide. It usually depends on the scale of its manifestation.

I feel your situation is manageable. You are empowered now because you see through this person's techniques. The crucial thing is not to give into fear as this feeds the negativity.

CHAPTER TWO:
Good Luck/Bad Luck

Subject: **Improving Your Luck**

Aura Soma Bottle # 78 (Divine Rescue- Violet/Deep Magenta) resonates to the energy of the Ace of Pentacles the major money card of the Tarot.

Dear Sarah
How can I improve my luck? I feel I may be cursed with bad luck. Nothing seems to go right and whatever I set my heart on fails.

You really must lose this negative thinking! You are not doing yourself any favours by carrying around this burden. Leave that passive state behind whereby you feel that life is something that happens *to* you. You have a lot more control and power to make things happen than you realise. The mind is like a cinema projector, and tends to reflect back to us on screen, the reel that is playing in our heads. So do make your personal movie a good one.

I do appreciate that it is a difficult adjustment to make. The development of this kind of consciousness is not easy. It is indeed a road full of tests and you must really *want* to develop and change on a deep level.

Admittedly it takes a long time to wake up with the feeling that you have creative control of your life. And of course it may never happen this time around. But do be reassured there are very definite steps you can take to improve *this* life's quality and energy.

Fundamental and personal change is a scary concept in many ways. But it is an exciting spiritual journey that will take you to interesting and challenging places. Surrender of control is the central paradox of this path. For only when you have actually given up, and surrendered to the situation, does the magic kick in.

Giving up selfish desires, thoughts, and ideas is the very powerful route towards being given everything you ever hoped for. But it must not be the motivation of your quest, or you will surely fail.

If you have a strong faith and belief in God or the Divine world all the better. Even on a psychological level handing your life over to God's better judgement can be a great relief. But for all the control freaks out there it is a daunting prospect.

What if there is no God, or angelic guidance and protection? How do I know that what a psychic suggests has any substance to it? This is where the leap of faith enters the frame. Nothing is achieved in life without a leap of faith, or several. The good news is that generally the Universe rewards us directly in proportion to the level, height and depth that we jump. Courage is everything. A fundamental and innocent, but not naïve. Faith will take you through life's trials.

Something to believe in, is of course very important for our psyche. The mind that expects negative events, persecution and misery will get just that. But the mind that believes, trusts and exercises Faith in the midst of suffering will be truly rewarded. This may all sound a bit abstract and overly spiritual. But believe me you will see practical results. It is a realistic approach to boot. It just depends on your perception of reality.

So suspend judgement and give these other dimensions a look-in. We all have guides and Angels to talk to and protect us. All you have to do is ask. It actually does not really matter if you believe it or not, just take the leap and see what transpires. I guarantee you that synchronicity will then begin to happen in your life and before too long everything will fall into place. But first you have to let go into the void. It is scary but your Guardian Angel will hold your hand and truly rescue you. Be careful not to worship your angels and guides though. Save that adoration for God him/herself. Develop the innocence of a child once again, and Life's magic, charm and mystery will return; or arrive. This applies to you whatever your circumstances. No one is beyond redemption. Ever!

Subject: **Winning Money**

Aura Soma Bottle # 10 (Go Hug a Tree- Green/Green) resonates to the energy of the Wheel of Fortune. Bottle # 78 (Crown Rescue- Violet/Deep Magenta) corresponds with the Ace of Pentacles.

Dear Sarah
I need your help and advice. I have a problem relating to winning money. I have no luck. I try hard but I just cannot win big amounts.

You will be glad to hear that in the long term there is peace of mind for you both romantically and financially. But you really must get on with daily life, and not build castles in the air, particularly when it comes to winning money.

One of the unwritten rules of the house regarding gambling, is that the house always wins. This is not actually correct, and being psychic certainly increases your chances of a win. But there are many people out deludedly there walking around with the belief that their numbers will hit the jackpot. If it is in your destiny to win, you will do so; and of course you have to be in it to win it. But as with everything, balance and a grounded sensible approach is the key to success.

I meet many people who have been told by psychic readers that they will win money. Unfortunately I usually have to get practical with them, and be the boring Virgo who dishes out a reality check.

We all have to have hope, and there is nothing wrong with believing in luck. However, although some of us will win, not all of us will. I think it is irresponsible that some psychics claim to guarantee the jackpot for their clients. Of course such information is good for their business and feeds our dreams. However, until the money is in your bank account I say, do not believe them. Certainly do not make life-changing decisions however convincing the information. I have heard of people re-mortgaging property or taking out loans, which is to say the least blindly trusting.

It is important to treat gambling as an entertainment, until the event of winning becomes a reality. However the Irish are a lucky nation, and someone has to win. We all have numbers that resonate to our energy, so trust your intuition at all times. Alternatively, simply do the quick pick so the lotto fairy can jiggle those balls in your favour.

If it is your destiny to win you will do so, but I am not willing to tell you whether it is or not. That kind of information jinxes a win before you even begin. For this reason the quick pick is about the most responsible way to place a bet. It makes us appreciate the chance aspect of gambling and does not lead us into major depression when our personal numbers fail us. It is important for you to relax and stop trying so hard. I would say if you have to gamble, do the quick pick and do not even read your ticket. Remember to *check* it though!

Subject: **Bad Luck**

Aura Soma Bottle # 19 (Living in the Material World- Red/Purple) protects against negative or poltergeist energy.

Dear Sarah
You really are my last hope. Please try and help. My alcoholic husband passed away two years ago. Since he died all hell has broken-loose and everything has gone wrong. My old home almost caved in so I sold it very cheap. But now this home is falling apart. I am worried about my children also.
Your husband's life path did not provide an easy ride for any of you. I feel that many of the incidents that have happened since his passing are his way of saying "I am still here you know!" The series

of bizarre events has been his way of keeping up a link with the family. You might comfort yourself with the thought that he has a perverse sense of humour.

I do not want to alarm you, but there is a need for peace to descend at this point. Angelic assistance is at hand so that his passing into the light will be complete. Healing is crucial for you all. It is important that you and your loved ones do not buy into theories of sabotage and bad karma. This negative expectation in itself draws in disruption. So, do lose your fear, and light a candle every evening until you feel peaceful in the home. I will attempt to help the situation energetically for you.

I know that priests have been in to bless the house and you have been lighting candles ad infinitum. But what I need you to do is use just one thick church candle as a way to link with the healing that I will do. Light this at 6pm every evening, and I feel that after five nights much of the energy will have cleared. You do not necessarily need to move from this house, though I would recommend that you redecorate and brighten up the front room in particular. Do not hold the belief that someone has put a spell on you. This is the kind of thought that enhances the effect of such things. Do not buy into this darkness. Be at peace.

There is a lot of disturbance in the minds of your sons, and in the energies of your home. Any household where all the electrical appliances have failed is a focus of psychic activity. Your family is very intuitive and psychically aware. However there is a danger that you will become ungrounded if you ruminate on the detail of past events. Do not give this mischief a foothold. If you want to move, then do so but I do not feel that you will have to. Certainly do not let these events drive you out of your home. The only answer to these problems is healing. The property you live in is built in a very energetically loaded area. Put your stamp on things and expect to be released.

Burn incense sticks, smudge with white Californian Sage, and bring natural quartz and Hematite into the home. Smudging would be very effective, so buy or order a sage stick. I actually feel that the candle trick will work so use these other methods as back up only if necessary. Most importantly: be at peace, and pray. Prayer works.

CHAPTER THREE:
Psychic Finances

Subject: **Lottery Numbers**

Bottle # 78 (Crown Rescue- Violet/Deep Magenta) resonates to the energy of the Ace of Pentacles a major money card.

Dear Sarah
I am a senior citizen. I live in a small rented council house. I have severe financial and some health problems. I am 69. How can I improve my standard of living? I have an interest in natural remedies, but treatments are so expensive. Things are very hard at the moment.

I can see that part of you has a wish to win some money, and why not? You are obviously carrying a lot of stress and worry about your survival. This is not helping your health. I believe that the battles in your head are the cause of your ill health. There are things you can do to help yourself.

Do you play Bingo? This might sound strange but I feel you could be lucky with Bingo. I do not mean that you must now rush out and buy scratch cards and lottery tickets, but there is the possibility of a small win. Use the numbers 10, 32, and your father's date of death. Also use the age at which you were at your happiest. Think back to significant dates. There was a special family gathering you particularly remember, so pick a number that connects to that. Make sure that you do the lotto-plus as well with these numbers. I would be surprised if you have not won some money by the summer. Trust in the angels to provide for you. Miracles do happen.

I actually think there is a new romance for you. I sense a new lease of life if you can relax and stop worrying. Why hold the belief that your future must be bleak? It is never too late to start life afresh. Keep a church candle by your bed and pray for help. Do not fall asleep whilst it is a light, but if you trust your guardian angel and ask for help, you won't recognise your life by this time next year. Bring some colour and brightness into your living space. The colour yellow is very healing for you, so perhaps buy intense yellow light bulbs. I sense that a church group that meets during the day will bring you companionship and new friends. Flowers also seem to play a significant role in your future. Had you thought of attending an evening class?

You do not need to struggle energetically through the rest of your life. There has always been enough food on the table and there always will be. You are a survivor. Do not be afraid to spend money. If you spend freely on the things that you need and desire your money will return just as freely. It is those who keep a tight purse and expect to struggle that remain tied.

Money is an energy that needs to come and go. If you hoard it and hold onto it then stagnation sets in. It is important not to begrudge spending. Why always head for the discounted goods in the supermarket? You deserve the best, so do not feel guilty about treating yourself even is it feels like a risky action. I do not mean that you have to become reckless and stupid with money, but do relax a little. Twinkle your way onwards and upwards. The little fairy folk will provide. Incidentally the numbers 1, 4, 7, and 11 come up regularly in the three Irish draws, as do the combinations 10, 20, 30, and 30, 49, 50.

Subject: **Cursed Re Money?**

Aura Soma Bottle # 19 (Living in the Material World- Red/Purple) will help financially and also protects from negative energy.

Dear Sarah
My first marriage was a complete failure and was annulled. Will I get a woman? Also I am owed a lot of money from a small insurance company because of an accident. Am I cursed? Everything I do seems to come out wrong. If your words are true I will buy you a new car!

It appears to be a common belief in Ireland, that the power of a curse can devastate lives. But what about our other legacy – a belief that the universe and God, hears us when we pray? How about moving beyond repression into faith and trust? Really the power of bad luck is wrapped up in the thought time we give it. Your mind has been programmed into expecting that everything will go wrong, and so it does. This demonstrates the power of the mind. Although we cannot not escape our destiny, at the same time we are co-creators of it. Assume responsibility for your life, and begin to manifest good things. At times we all walk around believing that life is something that happens to us. We have all been there: battered by circumstances with no way out. But believe me, there always is a way forward. 'This is the first day of the rest of your life' is a time worn expression that just happens to be true. It is possible to find peace and serenity alone, never mind with wife no. two.

You have battled with a lot of difficult circumstances, and you will find happiness if you concentrate on relationships with family and friends. Women are not commodities, so lose the fixation on "finding a woman". If you concentrate on respecting all those you meet, you may be surprised. There will be a court settlement in your favour, but it won't happen until you give up fighting. There may be big changes in your life but only if you surrender to the universe and expect good things to happen. This may sound flippant and naïve, and I do not mean to belittle your suffering. But, if you begin to pray, and trust your guides and angels, the miracles will begin to happen. That is a promise.

Subject: **Debt And Psychic Phone Readings**

Aura Soma Bottle # 19 (Living in the Material World- Red/Purple) is very supportive to those with financial problems. Bottle # 38 (Troubadour- Violet/Green) resolves spiritual illusions and helps you come to terms with betrayal and deception.

Dear Sarah
I am very heavily in debt. I am addicted to readings on the phone. I have been told that I have a connection with a famous man, and that we will be together. Is this true?

Unfortunately it is too late for me to warn you to be careful financially. You will manage to repay the debts, but you will initially need to borrow the money from a family member. The bill is in your father's name so he will carry the burden of this until you can repay him. I should point out that psychics-on-line are legally obliged to remind you of the cost of a call. Technically they should not allow the call to extend fifteen minutes. They should also watch out for people phoning obsessively.

You do of course have a choice. You do not have to phone. Having said that it is very seductive to be told something exciting and sensational. You want to believe it, so you phone repeatedly to see if the message is the same. This is how unscrupulous people make money. They have no problem exploiting your vulnerability. Some "card sharks," are excellent psychologists and have perfected the art of mind reading. These people are not necessarily psychic. They are trained to interpret the cards and keep you on the phone. Do not forget there is a boss behind this facade looking to extend his profit margin.

To be honest you would be well advised to find one person that you trust. It is easy to get waylaid if you take the advice of too many psychics. You will eventually start to hunt around for the reading that you like. This is quite literally paying someone to tell you what you want to hear.

Many of us do not have a true understanding of what it means to be psychic. We might have a naïve tendency to trust anyone with the ability to shuffle a deck of cards. What is the point of a reading if it is not accurate? In the wrong hands this stuff can wreck your head. Guidance that has no grounding in reality is irresponsible and dangerous. It is possible for your own expectations to show in a reading, so it takes wisdom to decipher the message.

When someone feels they have a connection with a famous person this is usually a karmic issue. Such readings can have a persistent life of their own. They are powerful, but ultimately damaging. A lot of what passes for psychic ability is in fact a mixture of auto-suggestion and projection. There are very few psychics in Ireland, even in the world you should trust yourself to; I can count them on one or two hands.

Subject: **Making Money From Psychic Ability**

Aura Soma Bottle # 65 (Head in Heaven: Feet on Earth- Violet/Red) is a clairvoyant's bottle. Bottle # 78 (Crown Rescue- Violet/Deep Magenta) opens the third eye. Bottle # 33 (Dolphin- Royal Blue/Turquoise) is very creative and inspires psychic ability.

Dear Sarah
Do I have psychic powers and can I develop them? What does it mean to be psychic and will I be able to make money from this?

There are many misleading ideas about what it means to be psychic. There is a sense in which we are all in-tune – we all have a mind that inspires our imagination and we all have our own special moments of heightened intuition.

These reflexes can be trained and the mind muscle can be flexed and toned in much the same way as the physical body. However, some people are more sensitive to unconscious messages than others, and are naturally intuitive. Those we call psychic have these gifts in greater measure. They are open and receptive to the language of symbols, and have skills of interpretation that translate the message.

Left-brained thinkers have a tendency to dismiss feeling responses, and only connect with what is visible or demonstrable. Those with "doubting Thomas syndrome" require empirical evidence for everything. They are inclined to line up the psychics in order to shoot them down at the first signs of ambiguity. Correct insights are dismissed as coincidental, and uncertain answers serve to reinforce their own superiority. This is the kind of mentality that expects a psychic to always catch her taxi, get to her appointments, and to win the lotto every week.

Seriously, knowing that something is going to happen is not the same thing as being able to stop it. Psychics are not divine. Foreseeing an event does not always guarantee us control over it. Ignorance tends to assume that psychics are forewarned about everything. Contrary to popular belief we are not always "switched-on." If we were, we would burn out within a week.

Psychic energy, whether it is used for healing or for relaying messages, is very intense. Working in this field has a price and is not to be undertaken lightly. You are setting yourself up for ridicule by those who do not understand. Even people's curiosity produces a difficult energy – you are caught between trying to explain and proving your own worth.

The true value of this work is for those who connect with you from a spiritual perspective. There is no sense of being on trial, and the genuine need for help validates the quality of what happens. If psychic ability is belittled, the messages received reinforce the expectation – is it really important who wins the football or the 3.25pm at Leopardstown? Our higher guidance is not interested in proving itself. Some things are a question of trust. Grace is generous when she is received not questioned.

Incidentally, money is not the correct motivation for this kind of work. It is really a calling rather than a vocation.

Subject: **Debt And Borrowing**

Aura Soma Bottle # 19 (Living in the Material World- Red/Purple) will help the sun shine on finances in the future. Bottle # 78 (Crown Rescue-

Violet/Deep Magenta) corresponds to the tarot card Ace of Pentacles which is a major money card.

Dear Sarah

I'd be very grateful if you could help me in any way you can. I'm in great financial difficulty. I cannot see any light at the end of the tunnel. I'm just an ordinary person in a dead end job. I owe £ 25,000 in debt. I'm at my wit's end. I need to get out of this mess very soon, or I don't know what will happen.

There certainly is a lot of stress in your life because of this debt. But you are not totally to blame. The financial institutions agreed to lend you the money, so they have to accept some of the responsibility for the transactions.

Lending money is how they make money, and do remember that they are insured against bad debts. They lent you money because they saw evidence that you could repay it. Amenable as banks can be, they do not hand out money for the sake of it. They must have believed you could repay your debts.

Please do not panic. There are things that can be done to ease your situation. I think that you should take financial advice about the money that you owe. Talk to the financial adviser connected to your bank. This person will help you to prioritise the debts, and believe it or not will show you how to save.

You need to declare your problem and then get practical about clearing the debts. Demonstrate your intention to sort the situation out to the customer services that handle your accounts. Alternatively, if you find an advisor to handle the debts, they would be responsible for communicating with the creditors. This does not inevitably mean bankruptcy rather you are enlisting legitimate help. People are allowed to come unstuck. It happens. The real test is how you handle it.

There are things that can be done energetically to attract abundance. Notice I do not say money. This is an important distinction. Sometimes we go wrong by focusing on the wrong priorities. Why tell yourself you are an ordinary person. Is that all you have decided you want to be? Do not limit yourself or undermine yourself with negative thought. Positive thinking really does help to turn the trickiest situations around.

Citrine is a crystal that attracts prosperity, and Mother of Pearl beads are very lucky. Make sure that your living space is free of clutter and keep the toilet seat down – this prevents finances being needlessly flushed away!

Lucky lottery numbers for you, are your Mother's birthday; the two digits of her age added together; the number of your childhood home; your favourite age; Number nine; and number two. Also go down to the nearest garden centre and buy as many Jade plants as you can afford!

Subject: **Psychic Lotto Numbers**

Aura Soma Bottle # 43 (Creativity- Turquoise/Turquoise) helps free a person up from illusion and futile pursuits, but also supports genuine outlets for the expression of creativity.

Dear Sarah
I'm so upset. I was told a few years ago that I would win big money. A Galway psychic gave me the numbers. Is this going to happen…or have I been a mug? Can you help me with numbers?

I know this scenario only too well. I have met a number of people who have been told they are future winners of the Lotto Jackpot. Certainly someone has to win. But I usually find that those who have been so advised have lost their freedom to a great extent. Dreams and hopes are important for all of us. We would lose heart, faith and purpose without them. However there is something quite destructive about hearing you may win large amounts of money. It has happened to me so I know what I'm talking about! When you hear from a reliable source, or the information is presented in a convincing way, you believe it. I am not saying this type of prediction is inevitably wrong. In fact I do win very regularly with 3 or 4 numbers, but a big win will arrive at some random point, out with my control. I do at least have some control in sensing numbers that are hovering to hit soon. So that is something.

However, it is very destructive to rely on this belief in a practical sense. *Never* act as if you have already won! You need to switch off to the idea, as you have become too dependent upon it being correct. This is not a healthy state of affairs. You may in fact even block your luck by being so fixated.

It was an understandable, underlying belief in my family that gambling or winning money was not the way to approach banking! However, when I was 11 I had my first experience of "seeing" luck from a different perspective. I was at the school fete, and I put a small amount of money on a spinning wheel, "knowing" that number 5 would up. I remember telling my parents when I handed over their bottle of cheap Champagne. They discreetly mumbled something along the lines of "there, there," and I recall feeling perplexed and short-changed by their reaction.

Similarly at a low-key show biz party, Guggi, one of Bono's best pals, was spinning a small roulette wheel for fun. I totally freaked him out, when three times in a row my predicted number 6/red kept hitting. He told me I would have been a very rich woman, had we only been in a Casino! Even more annoyingly, at one time I had all the numbers for the Irish Jackpot of 1.5 Million (which I had dreamt, and had been doing for a couple of weeks). But I missed doing them on the night they came good – I am still here to tell the tale! These stories give food for thought. Yes, people *do* win and have luck. But it is what you do with the *expectation* of winning that counts.

Money is to be loved and respected as a health energy. But negative approaches to its use, can be potentially destructive .Many of us carry quite limiting beliefs about money. However look at Philip Berber, who spends millions helping the poor of Ethiopia, and you realise that wealth in the right hands is positive. You may then wonder why I did not win that day, as the funds were for a deposit on a Dalkey healing centre. Perhaps I was not ready for that responsibility. Who knows? Destiny is a funny phenomenon.

My point is you could go mad believing in this stuff, and relying on it. Get on with your life in a day to day sense and be content within yourself. That' i what counts at the end of the day.

Money is an energy and expression of exchange. All things financial are relative anyway. It just depends on the scale with which you're working. It certainly does not buy you happiness. There is always a price to pay whether you are rich or poor. Think of all those celebrities who crave privacy, but cannot walk out of the door without checking with security. You may wish for a slice of what they have? Think again! A lot of us hanker for what we do not have. Is it not better to work with what we do?

Subject: **Silver Spoon Dilemma**

Aura Soma Bottle # 81 (Unconditional Love- Pink/Pink) helps with self-acceptance and the acceptance of others without suspicion.

Dear Sarah
I am worried I will never be happy. My parents always had high expectations of me when I was younger. And I always felt I had to prove myself. I am afraid that every new woman I meet will be after my money and status.

Poor little rich boy! Unless you want to end up moping, paranoid and lonely I suggest you give love a chance. Never mind your wallet, all humans need to feel loved, cherished and cared for. It sounds as if love often came with a price tag in your house. Now is the time to give into passionate emotions without keeping a running list of checks and criteria. Give life a whirl! Go with the flow and see where the Universe guides you. Be open to new opportunities and relax about what people want from you.

Unfortunately you have been programmed to listen to the cliches. Not every woman you will meet is primed to be a gold digger. Some of us value the healthy status of love, and companionship more highly than a big wallet. You must lose the expectation that everyone is thinking about your bank balance.

It is sad that your self-esteem has been so undermined by materialistic thinking. Your identity has become wrapped up in your gold card. Flashiness, Ferraris and choppers only do it for some women. The rest of us value the real thing. You are in danger of jeopardising your own happiness through stupidity.

Because you have status, and "old" money, your consciousness has inherited the belief that a lover may be more interested in your wad than your heart. Your parents certainly have this antennae well developed. Rightly in one respect; superficial chicks do exist. But I do not think they are quite as common place as you imagine - particularly not in Ireland. It would truly be a shame for you to miss out on a genuine expression of emotion and feeling. So stop blocking your pathway to love and life, before you even get started. Give people a chance to get real and do not give into paranoia and mistrust.

Sometimes these conditions are brainwashed into rich kids as a form of control. This kind of arid atmosphere reeks of emotional poverty. Riches come in other guises, and money certainly does not buy happiness or integrity.

Underneath it all you are highly intuitive. You have just been programmed to think in a particular way. There is no need to be on your guard quite so much. For, by carrying this negative expectation, you are attracting just the type of person you are trying to avoid. Irony has a sense of humour. Lose the negative thinking and chill out a bit. Perhaps you need to do some soul searching and get more of a sense of who you are and what you are looking for.

Being born with a silver spoon in your mouth is a mixed blessing. Security, caution and paranoia are unfortunately part of your legacy. I am not condoning irresponsible behaviour of course. But I think the best way for you to find true love is for you to first find your true self. Travel is a great way for you to find freedom and experience many cultures. You need to lose the lad-on-the-prowl vibe and give yourself some personal space.

A stretch of time alone at this point in your life is invaluable. Do not fall into the needing to be in love all the time trap. Treasure the real things not the trappings.

Money, status and power are seductive but they are no substitute for love. Join in the primal scream and do not be afraid to experience life, along with the rest of us.

Subject: **Lead Astray Financially**

Aura Soma Bottle # 79 (Ostrich Bottle- Orange/Violet) helps to overcome deception, especially spiritual folly.

Dear Sarah
I am hugely in debt because I listened to bad advice. Is there a way out of this mess? Why was I so stupid?

Firstly, you need to do some soul searching. What are your deepest beliefs regarding money? Do you feel deep down that you have a right to be prosperous and abundant? I might be sounding overtly American here; but I believe that our thoughts and beliefs very much shape our reality.

The external world is a diverse amalgamation of energetic thought-forms that have finally grounded. So what are your beliefs and how are they reflected in your daily life?

A lot of us feel there is something inherently wrong with financial fixation; and yet we strive towards a goal where money is no longer relevant, in that we no longer have to worry about it. We all hope to win the lottery – well a lot of us do. What then? Will everything be fine and dandy in your world? You may have no financial worries, but many will tell you your problems are just beginning.

It is important to look beneath the surface. Are you caught in a trap because in some way it is more comfortable than being free? That may seem to be the strangest question, but some people are actually afraid of the amount of liberation a windfall brings. Imbedded in the nation's psyche is an unconscious (or conscious) belief that money is the root of all evil. Its accompanying belief is that poverty and hardship are in some way noble.

Certainly in the past vows of poverty, along with vows of silence and honesty were deeply respected spiritual journeys. Something has changed. In this day and age money counts for something. It matters; and it takes a certain honesty to admit it. If you do not have funds you feel destitute, inadequate and miserable. And if you do, an air of smugness or complacency may not be lagging far behind you.

But how to get real in this situation? Let me assure you it is all relative. Your circumstances directly reflect your legacy of belief: the hippy mentality recommends living as if there's no such thing as money. The city stock-broker eats, drinks, sleeps money and spends his whole life striving to make it. Those born with the golden spoon take it for granted and may not even respect it. And the new money millionaires may end up feeling so guilty about their phenomenal resources, that they work tirelessly for charity, and want to save the world. Nothing wrong with that.

Where do you want to fit in? Yes you really do have a decision and responsibility to yourself here.

Get practical about your finances and take professional advice about your current situation. You do have the power and creativity to turn this around. It is highly unfortunate that someone has mis-led you by dangling the metaphorical carrot. But it is time to dice that carrot and see what you can come up with. Holding onto anger, blame and resentment will not help you move forward. That negativity will block your finances further. Claim your freedom and decide to trust once again. Just do not place your trust and faith in the wrong place. Learn from this lesson and never make such a mistake again. You gave your power away and leaked the life force out of your bank account in so doing.

Expect great blessings and abundance on your own terms. And use your inventiveness and creativity to dig your way out of a hole. All the best success stories have a down side at the start. May I recommend the book: *The One Minute Millionaire*, by Mark Victor Hansen?

Subject: **Legal Separation**

Aura Soma Bottle # 59 (Lady Portia- Pale Yellow/Pale Pink) helps impartiality and objectivity and brings a sense of detachment.

Dear Sarah
I am at my wits end! I have been married for 19 years, but I am sorry to say that things are not working out. We are going through legal separation at the moment but it is taking so long its driving me mad. Can you see any light at the end of the tunnel for me?

Your husband is a very stubborn and controlling man. He does not like the way you are entitled to half of the property and funds that you have built up together. Old fashioned may be; unfair certainly. As you have discovered when things do not go his way your husband will fight to the end on principle. You are quite right to question these principles but this man does not understand fair play. It is one rule for him and another for you. He is a man's man and his belief is that he should retain control of the funds and his family's future. You are not entitled to an equal share and so he denies you equal status. Fight for your rights even though you will emasculate him in the process. Justice will be served and if someone then has to bear the legal costs, that is the name of the game.

I know you are concerned about this apparent waste of money, but if he will not meet you half way then the judicial system will sort it out. I'm afraid that you will have to grin and bear the procedure. Your husband is hoping you will weaken and he hopes to wear you down by adding to your stress levels. It has become a battle of wills unfortunately. When this happens it is important to hand the situation over to the professionals and trust that justice will be served.

You certainly will not be out of pocket and you know that there are plenty of resources to share around. I believe that you will get further with your claims if you ask your lawyer to ensure the financial security of the boys. Try not to be greedy but make sure that your life style is maintained and that you have peace of mind into the future. You are worried about losing everything, so ask your lawyer the best way to proceed. See if the legal teams can arrange a settlement out of court as if this can be done sensibly it will benefit everyone. However, a courtroom appearance at this stage looks inevitable, so go with the flow and trust the process. I hope a last minute reprieve comes good.

Please reassess the schooling of your eldest son, as he needs the love and reassurance of his parents. I do not think boarding school will benefit him. He is sensitive and insecure, and needs kindness and understanding to develop and flourish. Knocking sense into him with a tough regime will not work. The comforts of home are especially important whilst his parents battle things out. I wish you well.

Subject: **Legacy Problem**

Aura Soma Bottle # 59 (Lady Portia- Pale Yellow/Pale Pink) will help you keep a sense of proportion about difficult events.

Dear Sarah
This time last year my best friend passed away. She left me everything but her brother made it his business that I got nothing. So many lies were told. I went

through a very bad time. Also I have a good idea that my husband came into money. I would really like to live somewhere else, and be confident that my health will hold up. I worry if I will be around to see any grandchildren growing up.

Your letter is about deeper issues than money and material security. It is about control. You feel you have no control over your life and the lives of your loved ones. You are concerned about your own well-being, and have many fears. This translates conveniently into financial worries and the desire to manipulate your environment. Why is it when loved ones pass away, we end up fighting and questioning their dying wishes? It is the responsibility of the legal system to ensure that a person's legacy is honoured. Believe me lawyers are paid to follow a will to the letter.

I do not believe that your friend's inheritance was watertight. The brother made sure that justice was done. This might be a devastating prospect for you, but if the will were meant to benefit you it would have done so. It is a time-honoured tradition that the benefactors of a will tend to be the deceased's family. I know that your friend was like a sister, but I think that you had certain expectations about the relationship. She probably felt quite dominated by people throughout her life, and the ambiguity of her legacy speaks volumes. Grieve for your friend not the money.

You say that you believe your husband has come into money, as your standard of living has improved. Why his secrecy? Again this is a control issue. You feel powerless because your circumstances are again being dictated by outside forces. Why do you not discuss a move of house with your husband? But do be sure you are not trying to rail against the status quo for the sake of it. To me your present house is fine, and I think your husband would be reluctant to move. I would not bother with another move in Dublin, but if in time you want to consider moving down the country (possibly to Wexford) this looks positive for you.

You also are frustrated at work, saying that you are not appreciated. I know you work hard, but none of us are indispensable. Really we work to earn our keep rather than to be praised. Having said that you do need more appreciation in your life. Tap into this from within. Do not expect it to come from outside. If we respect and honour ourselves others are quicker to agree with us. Do not expect to be hard done by and insist on some self-respect. This might sound rather unexpected, but you might benefit from a Reiki course and yoga would definitely be good for you. There is a new job offer for you, and overall you should begin to feel more relaxed, and content.

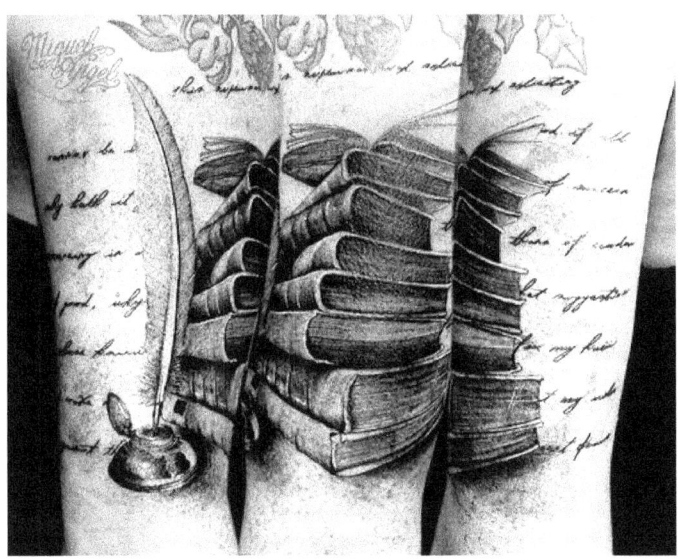

CHAPTER FOUR:
Things That Go Bump In The Night

Subject: **Haunted House**

Aura Soma Bottle # 19 (Living in the Material World- Red/Purple) helps to protect from psychic or poltergeist phenomena. Bottle # 94 (Archangel Michael- Pale Blue/Pale Yellow) resonates to the highly protective energy of Michael.

Dear Sarah
Is the house that I have lived in with my brother for 18 years haunted (We know of a cot death that sadly hit the previous tenants)? Also, are we cursed by a threatening chain letter that promised ill health and bad luck if we broke the chain? (Shortly after burning the letter I had to have a serious operation).

Firstly, I do not believe that the tragic death of an infant is placing you or your brother in any spiritual danger – such an energy, even if it were still earth-bound, would not be inclined to instigate any poltergeist or threatening activity. If you are concerned you should get the house blessed by a priest trained to carry out exorcism – please make sure of this, as it is possible to stir things up, if it is not done properly.

I do feel that the house is built in an active historical area and the air is thick with sadness. Your house is dark, musty, and damp, and this is contributing to your ill health. A lot of the energy in the house is trapped, and it feels oppressive. You should take action to freshen up the place – a grand clear-out and lick of paint should do the trick.

There are many things you can do to ensure the energetic integrity of the house. Frankincense heated in an oil burner is very purifying and lifts the atmosphere. Also, smudge the rooms with a smouldering sage stick will effectively remove negative energy. Do this repeatedly until you are happy with the results – particularly concentrate on the top floor and the staircase, as these are areas most susceptible to haunting. The Aura Soma bottle, Archangel Michael (no. 94) is highly protective, and no. 89, the Energy Rescue Bottle acts like a sponge to absorb negativity.

The chain letter has succeeded in making you very fearful and susceptible to autosuggestion – the priest's advice to burn the letter demonstrates his trust in divine protection. Burning is in fact a very effective way to purge funky energies. What is more, prayer is powerful, and is a strong weapon against the feeling of being spooked. I can assure you that God is well able for the antics of lesser entities. Your belief in the curse of the letter has given it power over you, so that you have come to expect misfortune.

We attract what we invest our energies in so it is important that you lose your vulnerability to the darker aspects of the spiritual world. You do have some control, and the resources to cope with fear – do not be a victim, and detoxify your house.

CHAPTER FIVE:
Eternal Triangles

Subject: **Love For Married Man**

Aura Soma Bottle # 87 (Love Rescue- Coral/Coral) should help support you and bring some clarity into this situation.

Dear Sarah
I do not know what to do. I am beside myself! I love a married man and I think he is interested in me. His wife recently had a baby so I think its hopeless for me and him. He blows hot and cold so I don't know truly how he feels. Will we be together or should I move on?

Oh dear, it looks as if you have fallen for the charms of a man who is confused. He is a lovely man with a lovely energy, and would not have deliberately led you on. However, he is uncertain of his own future, and you have unfortunately got caught up in the saga. This man is very loyal and committed to his friends, so even if he does have strong feelings for you, you will feel left out. It might be wise to sit down and think about what priority he gives you. At the moment you are nowhere on his list of engagements.

You have spent long years being patient and understanding of his situation and you are not someone who would normally hanker after someone unattainable. There is a strong bond between you and an understanding, even when you do not see him for weeks at a time. However, because you have been so kind, this man has not felt the need to make up his mind. He is a character who chooses to go with the flow of life, and to honour his commitments. So in many ways, much as he loves you, it would take a miracle to bring you together.

Having said that, when he blows he blows! There is a slight possibility that his domestic situation will get on top of him. He has married a clever woman who knows how to keep him. She is very cool: distant at the appropriate times; intense and connected when she has his attention. Underneath her aloof demeanour she is actually panicking. Because they have known each other for so long she has a strong sense he has fallen for you.

There will never be pistols at dawn with this scenario, but there is one thing she could not forgive - be very careful you do not get pregnant by this man. If you do she will throw him out. He will be all yours. Are you sure you want that? Do not forget he has stayed away from you despite himself. How encouraging is that for your future together?

Be sure of your own feelings and you will be ok. When you are true to your heart, you cannot fail. Eventually the truth wins out. So if you are sure, your focus and patience will be rewarded. You have kept your dignity, but perhaps it is time to wear your heart on your sleeve. Being dignified is not always the right way to get your man. You may actually be using correct behaviour as an excuse to avoid honesty, and a resolution to this situation. Take the bull by the horns and speak from the heart. At least then you will have clarity, and he can move on with or without you.

Subject: **Love Dilemma**

Aura Soma Bottle # 88 (Jade Emperor- Green/Blue) helps unravel complex emotional feelings. Bottle # 49 (New Messenger- Turquoise/Violet) heralds a new love connection, and supports young relationships.

Dear Sarah
I am a woman in her late 30's. I never married but have been in a long term relationship for many years. I am confused. A married man has been giving me mixed messages for 8 years. Nothing has happened but until recently I believed I was in love with him. Just before Christmas everything changed. I met a younger guy through work and have fallen for him. Help!

Oops! Your love life has got rather confusing. It seems to me that you are being challenged to assess what you really want from a relationship. You are trying to work out who your soul mate is. The married man is a bit of a slippery character. I do not like the way he has kept you holding on. He left you up in the air emotionally, and has not had the guts to speak plainly. This is really selfish of him, never mind his own confusion. It has compromised your relationship with your partner and you are now stuck in the middle.

Your feelings for the married man are very powerful, and there is a legacy of karma between you and him. He is in love with you, but cannot offer the hand of commitment. The past years have been absolute torture for you, but you have held onto your integrity despite the raging hormones. You deserve a break and a pat on the back.

The desire to get back at this man for so much wasted time and energy is quite strong. Do not bother. Even though you could embarrass him severely, it is better to walk away. I do appreciate that you have made major decisions because you trusted his advances. But we all make mistakes so try to forgive both yourself and himself.

Your long-term partner is a sweet heart, but you are more like brother and sister at this stage - nothing wrong with that. The compatibility and understanding between you is enviable. Even with the complex emotions regarding the married man you have remained good friends. It is probably the right time to talk plainly with your partner. You will never marry each other, but you have the kind of agreements that many married people would kill for.

You have the best of both worlds with this man. The freedom to pursue your own life and interests and the security of a happy home. However there is a vital missing ingredient, or several. There is no romance, passion or intensity between you. People say these elements disappear overtime, but I disagree. When you have a relationship that is both committed and passionate it is possible to maintain that in love feeling.

This is where the younger guy makes an entrance. He is everything you are looking for. Never mind the age-gap. If your soul mate appears and happens to be younger, you can be sure there is good reason for this. In any case how many forty-somethings do you know whom never grew up. This guy has an old head on young shoulders and is ready for love. Everything that you need and want in a relationship comes along with this guy. He blows apart the angst -ridden emotions re the married man, and he shakes up the complacency of your current partner. Apart from all that he is sex on legs, you would be mad to look anywhere else!

Subject: **Married Man**

Aura Soma Bottle # 87 (The Wisdom of Love- Coral/Coral) supports the turmoil of unrequited love and helps someone say "goodbye" to the past. Bottle # 47 (Old Soul- Royal Blue/Lemon) will help if the relationship feels like a karmic tie that you cannot break free from.

Dear Sarah
I am in love with a married man. He has shown signs over the years that he has deep feelings for me. I have tried to forget him but I find that I am waiting for him despite myself. He has a family and quite a prominent position – has he led me on or will he make a move?

This situation is sticky! You are right he has very deep feelings for you and he has done a lot of soul-searching because of it. He is a man with a conscience who loves his family. However he has a passion for you that buries deep into his soul - he does not know how to resolve the situation so he leaves it up in the air. Typical! It is important for you to get closure on this situation one way or another – so that you can get on with the rest of your life. In many ways he realises this and has stepped back in the hope that you will evaporate.

He is a lovely man – very kind and big-hearted. He genuinely loves you but the situation puzzles him, and sometimes he plays into it by showing some emotion. You are cool with him, and although he knows how you feel, he finds you tantalisingly self-sufficient. He is not convinced that you actually need him whereas he knows that his family does.

You are like a couple of teenagers skirting around an attraction that is both fascinating and scary. Unfortunately in adulthood the stakes are high – he does not want to make a mistake, and his reputation is very much part of his identity. He also gets bored quite easily so the fact that you have held his attention for so long does you great credit!

You need to talk to him - he would avoid you forever if you let him. You just need one chance to connect. You must be honest about your feelings and your vulnerability where he is concerned. This might be all that he needs to hear. There is an added complication in that his wife sprung an unexpected baby on him. We all know that this is the oldest trick in the book, and only works for so long. The issues that were there before the baby still remain – perhaps if you had spoken-up sooner things would have been different. You have both missed many chances to connect.

Do not underestimate his wife. She has a friendly public demeanour but she can be manipulative and controlling - she knows how to push his buttons and she knows how to keep him.

The morals of this situation are complex, but often it is better to be brave and leave a marriage that is for appearances sake only. Children have an uncanny way of working out the truth anyway. It is better to honour true emotions than to drag something out that has passed its sell-by date. This man is understandably trying to avoid unnecessary pain for himself and for his loved ones. However he is not following his heart, and will bury his head in the sand rather than make a move.

The attraction between you both is so overwhelming that he might even opt for an easier flirtation, or two, on the side, rather than go through the huge trauma of a divorce – which is what being with you would entail. It seems very much like you have a no-win situation. Your one hope is finding the space for genuine communication. Bear in mind that he will not instigate this – his best attempt would be a drunken lunge in a darkened corner. (Men can be cowardly in the face of Grand Amour). This situation could go either way – go for it and find out.

Subject: **Wiccan Relationship**

Aura Soma Bottle # 24 (New Message- Violet/Turquoise) to attract Soul mate. Bottle # 75 (Go with the Flow- Magenta/Turquoise) will help you accept things as they are and move effortlessly onwards and upwards.

Dear Sarah
I am a practising Wiccan but need guidance on the age-old problem of romance. I have been seeing someone since April 1999, but during the summer he strayed. Unfortunately we all work together. He is trying to end the affair with her but she won't let him go. Do we have a future or shall I look elsewhere?

Can you not do a spell to get rid of her?! I'm only kidding – I would not really approve of using any manipulation to get the result you want. If a man is not with you of his own volition, he is not worth it. This guy has the best of both worlds. He likes both of you for different reasons, and I do not believe he is trying to end it with her. He moved out of your home whilst still seeing her – what does that tell you? You could fight for him, but do you really want to hold onto someone who has treated you like that?

There is nothing wrong with you, but you do need to give yourself some respect. She will probably keep him by her undignified behaviour. He likes to feel loved and needed, and of course his ego is mightily confused. What to do? So many women so little time!

If you really still love him give him an ultimatum to choose between you. Otherwise I would recommend that you look for another job. Tell him this is your plan and check out his response. This will give you all the clues you need.

I do see a happy and passionate relationship that leads to marriage by the time you are thirty-three. There is also a child by the age of thirty-five. Your husband will be good looking, quite tall, and dark. His nature is fiery but he is also considerate and kind. He will be very romantic with you, and there will be no doubt about his feelings. Perhaps this frog you are dating will turn into a prince if you give him the fright he deserves. But he might not. You need to change the dynamic of the triangle you are entangled in. Your boyfriend has found he can get away with dating two women who are both afraid to lose him.

It is fear of being alone and insecurity that makes us accept less than we want. We tend to compromise because we believe our expectations might be too high. One of my boy friends once told me that a condition of him staying with me was that he be "allowed" to see his Ex on Sundays. I was that weak, I agreed. So take it from someone who knows. It is much better to be independent and strong than walked all over by a man you profess to love. Put yourself first for a change. If he is the right person for you he will not take such calculated risks.

Subject: **Unhappy Marriage**

Aura Soma Bottle # 99 (Archangel Tzadkiel- Pale Olive/Pink) helps transmute sexual problems linked with anticipation and expectations. It helps a person find delight in the moment. Bottle # 2 (Peace Bottle- Blue/Blue) brings deep peace that passes all understanding.

Dear Sarah,
I am looking for some insight into the future. I am very unhappily married to a man I never loved. About 12 or 15 years ago I met a man and fell in love. Of course he is also married and holds a high profile job. He tells me he wishes we had met 30 years ago. Please give me some advice.

Your situation is complicated! I do not feel that your lover is unhappy in his marriage, but I do believe that he is fond of you. He loves your company, and finds you light-hearted and refreshing. Both he and his wife have pressured lives and they are constantly on the go. They do not actually spend much time together. This might sound hopeful from your point of view, but essentially I think their marriage is stronger than he would care to admit. He is flattered by your attention, and when you chased him all those years ago he felt compelled to respond.

I do not think he is using you, but you are filling in the gaps in their marriage by still seeing him. This ironically makes him less likely to leave his wife, than if you were not around at all. I think she is quite a competitive and demanding woman, and you are a gentle but pervasive presence in the background. He is trapped by his conflicting urges for security and stimulation.

You appeal to his finer sensibilities and she is a match for him in the boardroom. He does feel guilty about the time he spends with you. He does not want to rock his boat and he has a lot to lose. She is the kind of lady who would take him on financially if she found out about this affair. So he feels intimidated by her and his livelihood and position are threatened if this scandal surfaces.

I think you can appreciate that it looks most unlikely that you will be together full-time. Do not forget that you are compensating for the lack of love and attention in your own marriage. There is a reason that you are looking at someone who is unavailable. There is a safety in that. It means you do not have to deal with your own problems. This affair is in fact keeping both marriages intact.

I do not think for a minute that you would leave your husband to embark on a life alone. You would not leave unless your lover arrived on bended knee. Believe me, even then you would not leave your husband.

Sometimes fantasy plays an important role in keeping us sane. It means we have an interesting diversion from the issues that trouble us. There is nothing wrong with a bit of escapism. However if we fail to hold onto some objectivity, our dream world can dangerously distort our perception of reality.

You are a mistress to a man you love. There is not really any other way to look at it, and when you take on this difficult situation you cannot expect an easy ride. He always will disappear for a few weeks after he is with you because you are *his* fantasy figure. He cannot bring you into his life full time because there is no room. You serve to keep him sweet and you enable him to have his cake and eat it too. I would not knock it if you can cope with the possible consequences, but do be careful. Accept the circumstances of this love and do not expect anything to happen. You might then be pleasantly surprised.

Subject: **Affair Possibility**

Aura Soma Bottle # 40 ('I Am'- Red/Gold) enables you to say 'yes' to life! It is very supportive of dynamic and expansive activity.

Dear Sarah
I am married since the late 70's and have been given a lot of pain by my husband. Perhaps I am afraid to leave him so I just get on with life. Nine months ago I met someone else. It is not like me to have an affair. Do I leave my husband? Is this other man any good for me? Will my son finish college?

I feel that the circumstances of your marriage are undermining for you. I think you should carefully consider a fresh start, not because of the affair but because you owe it to yourself. Your husband sounds like a selfish man who simply expects to be looked after, rather than someone who is relating to you as an equal. You are not obliged to stay. Your son is of age, and yes he should persist with college. His travels will work well for him and in time there is a happy relationship and several grandchildren for you. Relax about your son – he looks like he will do very well.

I think that a top priority should be to sort out your legal separation. You have the courage to do this, and I do not believe that you would be miserable on your own. Why not give yourself this fresh start? Your husband has intimidated and controlled you for long enough. Unfortunately I do not feel that he is open to resolving the problems between you. He will not change and he is actually oblivious to the depth of your hurt. Listen to your sister. She has good advice for you and will always be a great support. Why not take a girl's holiday before you make your decision? This will clear your head and get you focused.

I see much more contentment for you in the future. Enjoy your connection with the Taurus man. Taurus is very loyal and tend to honour commitments, so grab one if you can. Also they are the sign most compatible for a Virgo like yourself. A word of warning though, they are good at compartmentalising their emotions, and have an intense range of feelings for many people. This does not mean that they are inclined to be sexually unfaithful. But there is quite a tendency to wander emotionally. It depends upon your definition of infidelity I suppose. But if you can accept this character trait, a Taurus man is wonderfully sensuous; well worth the risk.

Incidentally, if you do separate from your husband you would legally be entitled to the house. However, you are financially secure in your own right, so you might prefer to offer the house to him. This would keep him quiet and he will be less likely to make other demands on your cash. Also I feel it is healthier for you to find a property you can nurture and make your own. Home is everything to a Taurus, so it is a wonderful focus and will help immensely.

The present house will just keep you energetically entangled in the marriage. You need a haven where you can relax and leave the past behind. Your husband will inherit a share of his father's property in time, so you do not have to feel guilty. You repay the debt to yourself – you have been compromising your own emotions for too long.

Subject: **Destiny Moment**

Aura Soma Bottle # 42 (Harvest- Yellow/Yellow) resonates to the energy of the 9 of Cups, the Wish card. Bottle # 34 (Birth of Venus- Pink/Turquoise) helps the communication of the heart, and supports a new relationship.

Dear Sarah
I'm really trying to put the past behind me. But recently I bumped into my 'EX'. I knew this would happen- I tried to avoid him. Now he's on my mind all of the time…again! He has someone else and so do I – 'Dilemma'.

Yes the "dilemma" seems to be affecting a lot of people at the moment. Being attracted to diverse energies, is part of life's rich tapestry. But there is indeed something quite powerful going on between you. A psychologist would say it is your mutual unavailability to each other which is the appeal. But you and he know different. The connection between you is so strong it is scary. It is as if you can read each other's thoughts- telepathy at its most sexy. Under the skin, you are true soul mates. You just have to realise it and stop resisting the inevitable.

I do not think for a minute it was a coincidence that you met up. Your paths are so linked that you could move to Timbuktu and he would find you. You experienced a destiny moment, that has shown you the shape of your future.

The very fact that you were actively avoiding each other only emphasises my point. The universe set this up to demonstrate that it is bigger than the both of you. It is time to be more compliant. We all know that it is not your style to break up a happy home; nor is it his. To an extent you have both made your bed. On this one. There is nothing you need to do to force the issue. Just exercise even more patience than you have already.

Destiny evolves naturally and organically. But there is nothing you can do to break its ultimate destination. Have you seen *Sliding Doors?* It is a perfect demonstration of what I mean. Yes, things get messy and delayed –that is inevitable too. But the end result is the same. Two people who are meant to come together will not be ripped asunder by peer pressure, bureaucracy or their own stupid resistance.

Things can shift and change in the meantime and get as complex as you like. But there comes a time where if you deliberately avoid each other for too long a universal thunderclap will occur to throw you together. If you insist on being stubborn to the point of complete denial it may be quite a sobering experience. You have been warned.

Be open to your future and trust that you will be guided. It will unfold as and when it is meant to. But do not expect it to be easy- I know you do not. In fact that is why both of you have ignored each other for so long. You know that a change of circumstances is not a nice thought. Believe me, you would be surprised how people adjust to your new circumstances.

Many know of the link between you already. But some deliberately work to keep you apart. They have their own reasons and their own agendas; and probably believe it is for the good of all that you and he never come together. Wrong. Ask yourselves, is it enough to be on each other's mind all of the time, and not be together? It is not a very friendly situation is it? To walk past or not even be brave enough to talk to someone you're madly in love with? Admittedly, it is all or nothing between you, so small talk is not an option. But how honest is this behaviour?

You both felt you had managed to forget one another. The Universe disagreed. It just shows that you can be as courageous and heroic as you like but love floors you every time.

Subject: **Affair Problem**

Aura Soma Bottle #88 (Jade Emperor- Green/Blue) will help you get a handle on complicated emotions within tricky situations.

Dear Sarah
I recently resumed an affair with the man I love. He is married but may separate. Will things work out for us?

They do say that you cannot help whom you fall in love with. This is certainly true. But the test comes in how you handle falling for someone who is unavailable. I will not bore you with the psychology of loving a man who cannot be yours, but needless to say it is worth giving it some thought. Perhaps you actually enjoy your independence more than you realise?

If you are honest with yourself, you will admit that your time alone with your child is precious, and you do not want anyone to invade that on a full time basis. So this affair suits you. I am not convinced you want this man in your life from day to day. Why not enjoy it for what it is?

This is a passionate intense connection and you are indeed soul mates. However, your man is entangled in a web of domesticity. Nothing wrong with that except that it does not give him what he needs. I feel sorry for him actually, as he is essentially an honourable man who has unfortunately fallen madly in love with someone other than his wife.

Life is not straightforward where matters of the heart are concerned. You have indeed fallen into a complicated situation. Enjoy your moments with this man, and do not expect any big change. The reason for this is that you then permit the energies of the situation to shift in your favour. If we interfere too much with the outcomes we desire we tamper with our destiny. Do not strive for the impossible and it just may be yours.

Subject: **Marriage To Gay Man**

Aura Soma Bottles # 27 and # 28 (Robin Hood- Red/Green and Maid Marion- Green/Red) support those with confusion re gender and sexuality. Bottle # 44 (Guardian Angel- Lilac/Pale Blue) will help you let go and not expect anything.

Dear Sarah
I married a man who turned out to be gay. Trouble is I made the wrong decision as another man who was keen on me then married someone else. I did not follow my heart. I love my husband and want him back, but I am now having an affair with the second man. What is the right thing to do?

Do you see the mess you can get into if you don't follow your heart! Be honest with yourself and work out whom is worthy of your affection. There are many types of relationship and many ways to express love. We all have the capacity to hold simultaneous emotions for several people. But this is where things get confusing.

Some of us get caught up in the belief that there is only one possible mate for us – our soul mate. The reality is there is so much opportunity particularly in modern society. We are all connected, we are all one and share the universal capacity to love and to be hurt by love.

No experience is a waste of time as every new person brings with them something different. Please do not see your marriage as a dreadful mistake. You were meant to unite with this man and express unconditional love for each other. Indeed you still love each other. The only piece that is missing now is the sexual union as he has admitted that he is gay. Here is proof that you love him in case you needed it.

If you chose you can still support him and love him and there is a possibility that you can make this unusual situation work. Married love is about expressing many different emotions, and it is not meant to be simply an outlet for our sexuality. However for many people sexual fulfilment is fundamental to a happy marriage, and many marriages fail if this important element is missing. These are the issues you have to negotiate with your husband if you want to stay together for reasons that are not purely sexual.

Many professionals would warn you that these are dangerous waters you are wading into. Are you sure you can handle an affair with another woman's husband whilst living with your husband who is out exploring his own sexuality? I can think of many easier ways to live!

It is surely the right time to take some personal space. Make the most of the freedom your husband is giving you. At least you are not making demands on each other. My strong advice is that you make a friend of your husband so that you can support each other with the huge adjustments you both have to make. Over these next two years life will take a different shape and you will be pleased with the long-term outcome.

Think carefully about the relationship with your lover. Step back and wait. If he is the right man for you he will take appropriate action. If he does not – Good riddance!

Subject: **Betrayal And Loyalty**

Aura Soma Bottle # 27 (Robin Hood- Red/Green) and # 28 (Maid Marion- Green/Red) support people with gender problems or sexual confusion. Bottle # 20 (Star Child- Blue/Pink) helps heal the inner child and is emotionally supportive in the midst of difficulty.

Dear Sarah
I feel very betrayed by a friend. She lashed out at me because I kept contact with her husband who turned out to be gay. They are now back together I have lost both of them. I tried to do my best and now I am lonely.

You have emotionally played both ends against the middle. There are dangers in being close to a married couple going through difficulties. It is a no-win situation. If they reconcile you are potentially ostracised, and if they stay apart your loyalties are torn. The likelihood of being stuck-in-the-middle is high. It is difficult to be genuinely supportive of both so you have to decide your strategy and be consistent. At least then you will have your integrity in tact if there is a difficult outcome.

The wife actually resents you, and was always jealous of your connection with her husband. However she is also quite needy, and you became a reliable mother figure. Her own mother is rather scattered, and eccentric and was always ambivalent about being a parent. You made her feel supported. Your natural warmth and availability made her feel loved. She is quite childish and immature, and expects ultimate loyalty from friends and family. She would expect you to break with anyone she has fallen out with, and because she was not aware of your continued contact with her husband she feels highly betrayed.

You are not entirely innocent in this situation - your natural joie-de-vivre makes you an instinctive flirt and although you are good company your friends are always on-guard when there is an attractive man around.

Your relationship with her husband annoyed your friend. She felt you were too familiar with him. When you all lived together she was threatened and sensed you were closer to him than she was. You played into this for your own reasons. As a couple they were useful babysitters, and they cushioned you from your own feelings of insecurity.

This complex situation is rich in emotional baggage for all of you! The husband also has issues that stem from his relationship with his mother and again you became a mother substitute - with some flirty fun thrown into the equation! You gave validity to the relationship of this couple – it was apparent to many people that he had gay tendencies, and this colourful trio that you made played into many levels of denial.

To be honest you are better off without this farce. It was both unhealthy and dishonest in many respects. You do not easily forgive emotional confrontation anyway. You are very black and white with your judgements. Just leave them to it. There will be other people to mother and flirt with.

CHAPTER SIX:
Domestic Violence/Abuse

Subject: **Aggressive Husband**

Aura Soma Bottle # 28 (Maid Marion- Green/Red) prevents someone living the role of victim. Bottle # 69 (Sounding Bell- Magenta/Clear) will help someone find personal balance in extreme circumstances. Bottle # 80 (Artemis- Red/Pink) helps you to let go.

Dear Sarah
I am a married mother of 4. I have been very unhappily married to an aggressive man for the past 24 years. He is sapping all my energy. It is a full time job trying to keep my health right. Since I bought another property, he is treating me the way I always wanted. What should I do?

I strongly recommend that you move into your property. Your husband is only treating you properly to control you so that you do not leave. If you sell that house you can kiss goodbye to your freedom. You followed your deepest instincts by investing in another place. It was a survival move that you knew would mean safety for you and your children. Under no circumstances should you get rid of that bolt-hole. Even if your husband were to wine and dine you daily for the next ten years I would not advise you to sell. There is certainly a delay in your reading regarding legal separation. This situation has spanned the decades and it is not about love it is about control.

There are many women who love too much, who love the wrong man believing that it may all change for the better in time. I'm afraid that such aggression from a man who is supposed to love you does not bode well. Statistically only one percent of men who are violent towards women reform. Trust me, this is not a problem that will go away.

Your husband is deeply insecure and stressed, and probably does not admit there was ever a question mark over his behaviour. The blind spots and denial in such men are huge. They use those who love them and are dependent on them to play out their unconscious issues. Such anger and frustration is abusive when directed at others. There is no excuse for it. Whether you love him or not, I repeat. There is no excuse.

You have a responsibility to yourself and your children to make sure you all live in an environment that is safe and secure. What is the fear and uncertainty doing to all of you? You are very fortunate to have your own property, and it would be folly to surrender it. I guarantee you, that if you did this, your husband would revert to his original behaviour.

If you do pluck up the courage to leave, you will see a very vulnerable side to your husband. There could even be panic and tears. He may find a way to melt your heart in the same way as a small, lost child. Be strong. By moving into your own space you are reclaiming your personal power.

You are totally zapped of energy because you have handed over the control of your life to a man who leeches your life force. The only way to help the whole family is for you to act.

Tough love is called for, and the discipline to see your decision through. Do not relent. The only way back to yourself is to stay focused and determined. Are you sure that you love this man? What are you saying to yourself by loving a man who threatens you and abuses you? I will send you healing, but you also need to assume responsibility and heal yourself. Why not be free and liberated from this bondage? Allow yourself the fresh start that deep down you know you deserve.

Subject: **Abusive Relationship**

Aura Soma Bottle # 33 (Dolphin- Royal Blue/Turquoise) has a liberating energy. Bottle # 43 (Creativity- Turquoise/Turquoise) will connect you with your own creativity.

Dear Sarah
I feel I have wasted my 20s. I stayed with an abusive boyfriend for many years until a friend 'rescued' me. Now I cannot believe I got into that situation - have I ruined my best chance of happiness? I am in my thirties now and feel that I took a wrong turn.

Please do not think that you have wasted your life – fate has some amazing things in store. Although you may not marry you will find happiness with a charismatic, interesting man. There will be a son for you both. For the first time you will feel truly loved.

Do not punish yourself about your negative experience. There is a gift in every situation however traumatic. You now have huge empathy and understanding for those in emotional difficulty. I guarantee you that this will be used to great effect later in both your career and private life. You would make a talented carer and counsellor, and never again will you allow yourself to be a victim. This experience has strengthened you beyond measure and has knocked your vulnerability on the head for good.

People who abuse others are usually hopelessly insecure. They seek to control their victim in order to give their lives validity and a measure of security. The scary thing is, they are quite frequently intelligent – their manipulation works by undermining someone else's psychology. This can represent the complete disintegration of a once strong personality. The technique is insidious, and the controller creeps up on his prey virtually undetected. It is uncanny the way in which these characters are able to strip your defences so that you become totally reliant upon them. They have a way of making you doubt everybody, and they present themselves as the only person you can trust.

Do not blame yourself. This can happen to anyone unfortunate enough to get emotionally entangled with an abuser. You are naturally more cautious with new friendships, but that is not a bad thing. Your self-esteem has been shamelessly undermined, and the sad thing is the ex-boyfriend will never accept that he acted wrongly. Even as an eighty year old man, this guy will be attracting those with a victim mentality. Write him off as a bad deal. You deserve better, and you will get it.

Subject: **Violent Abuse**

Aura Soma Bottle # 28 (Maid Marion- Green/Red) help release you from the victim mentality. Bottle # 47 (Old Soul- Royal Blue/Lemon) helps to disperse the feeling of persecution.

Dear Sarah
I have known a separated man for 3 years, but the relationship ended because of the verbal abuse. He was also violent but always apologised. How do I get him out of my mind?

I am glad to hear that you would not contemplate going back to this man. Do you wonder why his marriage ended? It is quite clear why. I do appreciate it is a bewildering experience to love a man who is violent towards you. Your logical, rational mind knows that he is not good for you; and yet there is a compulsion to be with him; because, you love him.

A psychotherapist would of course point out the self-esteem issues that accompany loving a man who abuses you verbally and physically. But this insight does not particularly help you to process the pain. Having said that you may wonder why you attracted him in the first place. Energetically speaking we tend to draw towards us situations that help us play out our issues and hang-ups. But now I'm sounding like the psychotherapist.

I do realise that it is incomprehensible to you why this experience happened. The nature of this scenario is by definition unexpected and shocking. Violent men do have a compulsive aura that may be compelling as well as repulsive to us. Such relationships reel us into an obsessive co-dependency that can be difficult to break. We engage with the enemy because we think we might be able to help and because "we love them!"

This rationale turns a lot of women into victims. They end up in a situation that is virtually impossible to disconnect from without an extreme act of bravery. It is this dark fascination that keeps us in place. As well as the nurture/nature belief that we might be the one who can reform and change this man.

Violent attractive men bring out the fighting spirit in women who love "too much." For those on the outside looking in, it appears that the abused party is a weak victim who cannot break free. There must be some inadequacy and bond of need that means the balance of power is non-negotiable. Think again! Such assumptions can be way off the mark.

A lot of the women who love too much, are incredibly courageous, if not a little misguided. They have families to hold together. They juggle children, housework and the partner from hell. All in a day's work you might say.

Frequent apologies are of course part of this mutual arrangement. There is an agreed unspoken contract which means the momentum of abuse is difficult to break. We all readily say that if the man we loved hit us we would turn and walk away; until it happens. Deep down we know the behaviour is inexcusable and yet we maybe in an established and respected marriage. How then do we fend for ourselves?

It takes extreme courage to stay or go, so we settle for the slightly easier option. I can identify with the loneliness you feel. Be strong in your resolve to stay away; and never go back to this man. Violence and abuse are not expressions of love even if they are accompanied by an apology after the event. In fact they are expressions of male inadequacy, frustration and sheer temper. This lashing out and lack of control has nothing to do with love. I am sorry.

The brutal truth is that power and control issues do not a healthy relationship make. Under no circumstances should any one stay with a person who weakens or abuses them. It is a matter of mustering the courage to stay away. So keep him out of your head. There is healing for you and this negativity can be finally laid to rest.

Subject: Shall I Use The Gift?

Aura Soma Bottle #5 (Sunrise/Sunset- Yellow/Red) helps process the difficult experience of abuse.

Dear Sarah
I am psychic but do not use my gift as I find it brings with it too much difficulty. I was abused as a child and after a traumatic marriage I am receiving counselling to heal these issues. Will I be able use my experience to help others?

Quite a number of people who have psychic gifts have experienced varieties of abuse in their lives. In one respect this prepares them to help others cope with trauma but it also leaves a legacy of personal damage which needs to be processed first.

It is not possible to effectively counsel others until you have achieved a discernible level of development or integration.
What is really important is that you help and nurture yourself before you even contemplate trying to focus upon other people. It is quite ok to be selfish in these circumstances. You really have had a plateful of abuse so it is a testimony to your kind heart that you still want to give of yourself.

Sometimes women do love and care too much for everybody except themselves, so your challenge is to put a stop to this. Learn to put *you* at the top of your list of priorities.

To be honest it is quite an art form trying to develop healthy selfishness, especially when every reflex is programmed to help others rather than yourself. Such self-denial can unfortunately go hand in hand with a victim type mentality, which in turn invites the abuser to continue their destructive behaviour. The wake-up call arrives when the victim realises their vulnerability and shouts stop! The self-deception and denial that covers the tracks for the abuser up to that point is scary.

When you look back at what you put up with and it seems like it happened to another woman in another lifetime, then you will know that you are fully healed. This is not to say that you must deny what has happened. It is very important to receive the counselling or healing that makes sense to you.

Learn to listen to yourself and gain personal strength by saying no to abusive situations. Sensitive and kind people are unfortunately vulnerable to those in a position of power who do not have a conscience, so protect yourself and toughen up. The colours yellow and red in combination support those who have experienced abuse, and wearing pink promotes self-acceptance and unconditional love.

CHAPTER SEVEN:
Depression And Grief

Subject: **How Do I Get A Life?**

Aura Soma Bottle # 56 (St. Germain- Pale Violet/Pale Violet) helps the transmutation of negativity and is very supportive during depression.

Dear Sarah
Three months ago I was made redundant. I am now down and despondent. My sleeping pattern is disturbed and my appetite is upset. I am anxious and depressed. I have been avoiding going to my GP because I am cautious about taking medication. What are my alternatives?

Firstly, it is important to realise that depression is no respecter of status. It is an illness of the spirit that may affect anyone from the

Pope to the puppy abandoned at the roadside. In your case it is tempting to put this onset of the blues down to your redundancy. But in fact there are deeper issues relating to self-esteem that should be addressed. A healthy psyche does not depend upon the maintenance of a particular job. There are many paths to elevation: Buddhist monks spend lifetimes doing mundane repetitious tasks in the quest for enlightenment. My point as a spiritual healer is that depression may be tackled from a different angle.

Admittedly some patients are programmed to respond to medication. It suits their mentality. Others like your-self want to tackle the problem head on. Medication suppresses the pain and underlying causes of depression. True healing brings them out into the air so that the negative energy may be transmuted. Even one session of healing may shift a depression that is ready to depart. I have had many clients that got despondent with medication because they had an in built sense of its futility. Depression has so many manifestations. It respects our individuality and consequently feels different every time. A treatment that unlocks the demons in one mind may in fact compound them in another. This is the beauty of spiritual healing: it caters for the uniqueness of the client.

On a practical level, the crystal Hematite is very grounding, and helps us source the correct plan of action for survival. If your depression is caused by grief and loss Amethyst is indispensable. It is highly protective and helps us process our upset in ways that are not destructive.

There are now many flower essences available that address the causes of depression energetically. It is possible to be muscle tested for the suitability of various products. Then you are assured that the medicine exactly compliments your energy. Swimming in the sea is highly beneficial. It cleanses the body on a deep level, and this daily detox will boost healing.

With any depression it is a good idea to persist with exercise as this naturally elevates Serotonin levels. Finally, nothing beats a good cry. In the context of a healing session such a release of emotion shifts depression quickly. It is eminently preferable to months of pill popping.

Subject: **Depression And Worry**

Aura Soma Bottle # 42 (Harvest- Yellow/Yellow) is very supportive when afflicted with depression. Bottle # 25 (Florence Nightingale- Purple/Magenta) offers release from past disappointments.

Dear Sarah
I am on medication for depression. I'm a lone parent with one child, who I love so much. Her father left me but I'm getting on fine with him. Please send healing for my father who is very sick, and for all of us so that we may get through this difficult time. Will I meet someone who will love me?

You certainly deserve to be happy. You are a wonderful mother and you have coped admirably with the rejection of your ex. It is the right thing to maintain a positive relationship with this man. There is a happy marriage on its way for you after a time of grief and heartache. You already have experienced the worst times, and the medication has enabled you to function. Do seek out a healer if that makes sense for you, and it would be good to aim to stop the tablets soon. Check with your doctor to see if he agrees. Do not be afraid to cry and feel the sorrow of grief.

The homeopathic remedy *Ignatia* is brilliant support for the process of letting go of a loved one. Your father will always remain close to you in this world and the next. In fact he will be with you all the time, where now you have to leave the room and get on with your day.

Pray to your angels for peace and protection. The support of your family and the love of your daughter will see you through. When the time comes you will be relieved to know that your father is at peace. Our Heavenly Father has a wonderful way of carrying us through the journey of death. You will be aware of his love and care, and there will be a strong feeling that your father is in a better place.

Trust the timing of these events and surrender to divine will. There is no better way to be assured of getting on the right track. Your angels will bless you with happiness. I would not be surprised to hear that you had reconciled with your ex. But you have a choice! There is a strong relationship for you with a funny guy who has had some difficulties with his working life, but has a new job on the way. There is a passionate connection again in the future, and your father will see to it that the right guy gets through.

Do not feel a failure. You know that your daughter needs and loves you, and that whatever takes place your relationship with her remains a priority. She will return your love tenfold. Had you thought of getting a dog? I believe it is no accident that dog is 'God' spelled backwards! Unconditional love, devotion and loyalty. What more could a girl need?

Subject: **Depression**

Aura Soma Bottle # 56 (St. Germain- Pale Violet/Pale Violet) helps shift and transmute negativity particularly around the head. Bottle # 78 (Crown Rescue- Violet/Deep Magenta) is also very good for lifting depression when used alternately with # 54 (Serapis Bey- Clear/Clear).

Dear Sarah
I have suffered for twenty-two years with depression. I feel that the world would be a better place without me – I feel guilty and useless. Can you give me any advice on how to cope?

It is difficult to know how to advise you because a major feature of depression is the belief that no one can help and that nobody understands. Every case of depression is unique which makes sense as we all have different minds. There are as many types of depression as there are people experiencing it. This adds to the feeling that no one can reach or identify with you.

Indeed, every depressed person is right. It is nigh on impossible for someone to empathise unless they have been there themselves. This is why support groups are important; if nothing else they help confirm our belief that we are beyond help. I am being flippant because I have experienced the tricks that our minds can play with our judgement during depression.

The really crucial guidance for getting better is: learn how to be selfish. It is important to follow the rhythms of your body. If you cannot sleep at 5 am, so be it. Get up, and if you are tired again at 2pm go back to bed. You have a lot of guilt attached to breaking the rules that your mother taught you. Part of your challenge is to learn how to do your own thing.

Accept your condition, as this is the key to turning things around. If you feel depressed acknowledge it do not fight it – if you want to lie in a dark room feeling blue it is okay! This sounds rather corny but it works. You will find that your time lying on the bed reduces week by week. You will eventually have enough curiosity about life to want to make a cup of tea for yourself. When you want to do something savour the moment. It can be quite a Zen-like experience.

Even if your only joy is a hot bath and a cup of tea keep doing these things – slowly you will add other things to your list. It is true to say that if you act as normal eventually the emotions will kick in. Show willing with your daily routine and your mind will follow.

Of course make sure that your doctor is happy with the way that you are coping, and if you can connect with a designated support system, so much the better.

I can testify from experience that depression does pass. It is a challenging situation, and at times you feel fragmented. If you pull through there is not much else with which life can faze you. Potentially this kind of suffering leaves you with heightened compassion and sensitivity and the ability to help others. Incidentally there are special healing techniques which help to clear depression and other kinds of emotional distress. It is not just physical ailments that shift with Reiki, Aura Soma, and other kinds of healing.

Persistent or recurring depression is indicative of unresolved patterns and it is sometimes helpful to adopt a spiritual approach to tackling the problem. The church often refers to this experience as the dark night of the soul, and quite often it can feel as if you are under attack by a force beyond your control. It is worth seeking advice from a priest or religious leader, if this fits with your view of the world.

Prayer is also helpful. The one thing I remember from my experience is that everything fell away except a sense of God's presence. At one point he/she was quite literally the only thing left. This is a good foundation on which to rebuild your life. Gradually you will come back to yourself knowing that he/she is at the heart of everything.

Subject: **Obsessive Worry**

Aura Soma Bottle # 42 (Harvest- Yellow/Yellow) encourages the release of fear and inspires joy. It is very good at shifting anxiety states and depression. Bottle # 53 (Hilarion- Pale Green/Pale Green) helps clear and support hidden phobias and worries.

Dear Sarah
I am in turmoil. My husband has very strange mood swings that started at the same time as his new job. Often at night in his sleep he groans and calls on his mother. His subconscious behaviour is disturbing me.

My first reaction to your letter was that the poor man needs some space. He feels that you are monitoring his every waking moment. On top of that you have become distressed about his nocturnal habits. I do appreciate the anxious state that you are in but a lot of this is of your own creating. Surely all of us are entitled to some privacy especially in our sleep. A lot of unconscious issues are processed in our sleep, some of which would surprise us.

Just because he looks at you without recognition when half asleep, does not mean he does not love you. He is ageing, and has various health problems. His medication does indeed give his system a lot to cope with. On top of that he works hard, and does his best to make you feel loved and needed.

You should really be thankful for the commitment that he gives you. It is true to say that women are from Venus, and men are from Mars,' and that the language of love can shift over the years. However, he shows absolutely no sign of taking you for granted, which after twenty-three years surely deserves a medal? Have you ever noticed him get into a mood of his own volition? I think not – it is always in reaction to your questions. This man adores you, but he could use some privacy.

Learn to ignore the moments when he seems distracted or vacant. I feel that sometimes he keeps his physical difficulties quiet so as not to distress you. He suffers in silence, and your enquiring nature burdens him unnecessarily. I think you should relax. There is nothing sinister that he is hiding from you. Take your life together at face value. I do not feel that you need to second-guess this man.

Most importantly I think you need to work on your own independence. Learn to enjoy time apart. That way you will start to have more objectivity. It is very easy to get wrapped up in co-dependency, and believe that everything must be done together. However, this is ultimately stifling and unhealthy.

Sometimes women have to learn not to care so much. A lot of our perspectives go over a man's head! It can be quite useful to develop camaraderie rather than monitor everything from a romantic viewpoint. This man is surely your best friend. Why not give him some trust?

Subject: **Preoccupations: Death, Cutting, Depression.**

Aura Soma Bottle #16 (The Violet Robe- Violet/Violet) supports healing re the fear of death, and helps someone come to terms with a near death experience.

Dear Sarah
I used to suffer from severe depression but I went for counselling and now it's not that bad. The depression was mainly about dying and I often thought about taking my life over it. Recently a friend was killed in a crash, which brought it all back. Will I ever get over this?

It is a great shame to be so preoccupied about death at such a young age. But I do empathise with you, as I had a similar experience. A lot of sensitive people who think deeply and are of a philosophical bent go through this. Be encouraged, as it is a mark of your depth of character.

My father, a doctor, and psychotherapist, says that the best of us experience depression. If you come out the other side you are a better more discerning person. Difficult as it may be, look to find the gift in every situation. Life is not just about good happy times. Unfortunately we all have to face challenges and heartache in different ways.

The dark times make you stronger and give you a contrast experience, which heightens joy when it occurs. It would be disappointing if life were dull and bland. It is the drama of good and bad events, which gives us: a life!

A preoccupation with what you would do if various members of your family died is not uncommon. But it is quite unhealthy to fixate upon this issue for too long. If you find that such thoughts recur or persist you may have indeed have a depression that needs to be treated.

I will do healing to shift this negative energy for you. Use the colour lilac whenever possible and paint your room this colour if you can. If you can find a piece of amethyst crystal from a stall or shop carry it around as amethyst is highly protective.

Please refrain from cutting yourself, as this destructive behaviour will not bring you any answers. You are angry, frustrated and cross with life, and rightly so. What we have to face is not easy and death is certainly not easy. But there are good things out there as well.

It is now time for you to live your life to good effect. You have processed a lot of difficult thoughts and you have been brave enough to look at things that some of us never face. Well done you deserve, a pat on the back for having the guts to face the truth. Now you need to balance this experience and enjoy the rest of your time.

The reality of death is very different from the fear of it. God has a way of taking care of our exit even if we do not appreciate it at the time. There is a divine plan in place, and none of your loved ones will depart before they are meant to. It is not good to waste precious time by worrying about events that are in the future. The time is now. Enjoy every moment of your life. The difficult thoughts you have experienced will ironically enable you to do this. Instead of holding you back, or paralysing you with fear, the negativity will be transmuted. This means that everything will come right for you if only you expect it too. Along with the healing, positive thinking will turn your life around.

Subject: **Letting Go**

Aura Soma Bottle #10 (Go Hug a Tree- Green/Green) helps us to respect the boundaries of loved ones and to find our personal space. Bottle #87 (Wisdom of Love- Coral/Coral) helps us to process feelings of unrequited love.

Dear Sarah

I am married since 1945 and have three adopted children. My husband and I have been going through a very hard time these last 10 years. I am a really anxious person. I have strong feelings for my counsellor, and was devastated when he got married. A fortune-teller told me that she had never seen a reading like mine. Everything that could have gone wrong has done so.

Will you please stop blaming yourself for what is wrong in everybody else's life? Your three adopted children will find their own way forward, particularly as they are now adults. It is part of every young lad's experience to get up to mischief and to experiment with substances they should not go near. Obviously the degree of being bold will vary, but a youngster needs to privately work out his own boundaries. You can only offer your parental guidelines and appropriate discipline, then hope for the best. You are right obsessively breathing down the necks of your children helps no one. This is not another excuse to beat yourself up – what is done is done. It is now the time to move on with your own life, and surrender your loved ones to the divine parent in the sky.

It is really important for you to get to the bottom of your own heartache and sadness. Your counsellor will help you achieve this. It is very common to have strong feelings for someone who is helping you in this way. It is this man's job to ensure that his professional behaviour remains scrupulous. You are right, the fact that he got married is really nothing to do with you. He has compassion and feels empathy for your situation. It is not healthy for you to harbour feelings for him. I would actually recommend that you change your counsellor at this point, so do put in a request to that effect with the hospital.

It is actually possible to become too reliant upon those whose job it is to help us. Tough love at this point would buy you your freedom. You may no longer need to pour out your heart. My feeling is that you need healing and times of quiet and relaxation. Sometimes words are not enough, and a few sessions pampering yourself will work wonders.

I will keep you strongly in mind when I do my long distance healing sessions. You will become more independent and relaxed. It is important to find your own power at this point in your life. It will be a process that will naturally unfold for you. Start to have a bit of fun. When you are angry and frustrated express those feelings then move on. It is okay to cry. When you are depressed it is common to cry on a daily basis. The way through this is to accept this is the space you are in. Do not fight against the things that cannot be changed.

In the times we are living in it is so important to savour and appreciate the good things in our lives. We may not have all the things we ever wished for, but we do all have a measure of hope to play with. When I was depressed a cup of tea was the highlight of my day; it sometimes still is. It is the small things that count. I can assure you that the more you relish the positive things in your life, the more they will multiply. We attract to us the events and experiences we expect. So lighten your load and expect the best. That way you will bring some magic into your life.

Subject: **Bereavement**

Aura Soma Bottle # 26 (Humpty Dumpty- Orange/Orange) is very powerful for all levels of shock.

Dear Sarah
I am devastated my older sister passed away very suddenly. We all thought her husband would die first. He has been very unwell and she was never sick. What is doing on?

The shock of your sister's unexpected passing has hit you hard. So go with the flow of the devastating emotions. It is okay to feel angry, upset and frustrated. Please do express these feelings rather than attempt to be brave by suppressing them. Ugly, embarrassing emotional outbursts are better for your health than pushing down or ignoring your grief.

Unexpected deaths always inspire the bereaved to question circumstances with a string of "if onlys." It is a way of coming to terms with the impact of 'accidental' death. Understandably your whole system is reeling as a reaction to the event. You were all so involved in monitoring the complex health problems of your brother-in-law that this surprise is all the more difficult to come to terms with.

If it is any comfort to hear, the Universe/God often allows the stronger apparently immortal carer to die first, in order to pave the way for the terminally ill patient. This is especially true in close marriages where the sick person is holding onto life for the sake of their loved ones. Of course this is very human and understandable. Many of us do want to live as long as possible. The fear of death and what lies beyond only enhances our determination to hold onto life.

You have probably heard of the many accounts of near death experiences. These offer some hopeful evidence and prepare us for what the journey into eternity is like. Those who experience the bliss of these special moments never want to return to the physical body. But they are told that their time on earth is not yet done, so under duress they return. This is an immensely comforting thought for those thinking about loved ones that have passed on. They are surely in a better place.

The value we (hopefully) place on life is justified. But those who have watched loved ones struggle with illness and pain will often recount their relief when death occurs. This passage of life has equal weight and consequence as birth. It is part of the ebb and flow of Universal events, and should enhance our awareness both spiritually and emotionally. Many people can vouch for the peace that descends when someone passes on after a long illness. The release from pain, suffering and misery is tangible, but bittersweet.

But, as you are finding out, it is so much more difficult to come to terms with the loss of loved ones suddenly and dramatically, as if by accident. This is such a challenging adjustment to make. Trite as it may sound, time really is a great healer. And you will frequently find, when you have the benefit of hindsight, that the personality and character of the deceased often add up to the circumstances of their passing.

Perhaps our heart and mind comes to terms with the event by perceiving things in this way. But one thing is for sure, life is precious and to be respected. With loved ones resting in eternity, we owe it to them to value our time here on earth.

To make the most of life is the best legacy, inheritance and memorial statement possible.

Subject: **Clingy Co-Dependency**

Aura Soma Bottle # 90(Wisdom Rescue- Gold/Deep Magenta) will help you embrace your own confusion. Bottle # 32 (Sophia- Royal Blue/Gold) helps the deep release of fear and brings peace into the picture.

Dear Sarah
About two months ago I noticed that I was feeling very down in myself. I feel totally unmotivated and hate to be alone especially at night. My boyfriend has been brilliant, but I am very dependent and clingy, wanting to spend every single moment with him. Why has this happened?

Moderate depression is a very bewildering condition. We feel out of sorts but don't understand why. We still have a sense of ourselves and yet we are somehow alienated and disorientated. It is as if we are not engaging in life to our fullest capacity. Of course we go through the motions and put on a brace face, but inside we are vulnerable and weak.

Thankfully this kind of depression is not as crippling as severe clinical depression, but it still has a physical impact. It is common to cry at the strangest things and our own company is quite scary. This is because we suddenly have the weirdest feeling that we no longer know who we are. Psychotherapists call this an identity crisis. I call it a very unsettling head-wreck.

It is wonderful that your boyfriend is being so supportive and grown up about this. It is a good indication of his love for you. Time is the best healer of this condition. You will find that there are days when it is not so difficult to look at the stranger in the mirror. Every few weeks you will realise that you have made progress.

One day you will look back at this experience realise that it was the best thing that could have happened. Believe me, you will come out the other side of the tunnel a different but stronger version of the person you were before.

Unfortunately, the blues is fairly common for sensitive and creative people. It is usually the most interesting and complex people who struggle with depression. I know this thought is no comfort for you at the moment, but within two years you will look back on this time as a gift. You do need to be on a mild antidepressant for longer than a month, so do not be afraid to go back to your doctor. Sometimes healing helps to shift the energies of a depression that we do not understand. I will do some long distance healing for you.

I know that you want to identify the cause of your ill health, but there is not always a logical reason for depression. Quite simply, your Serotonin levels need a boost. The medication will sort this out, and moderate exercise is a good idea. This releases the natural endorphins that make us feel better. Cuddling up to your boyfriend will also help.

A word of warning though. There is the possibility of pregnancy fairly soon, so take precautions if you are not quite ready. Relax and enjoy the security of family and friends and this time will pass.

CHAPTER EIGHT:
Dilemmas

Subject: **Moving Home**

Aura Soma Bottle # 63 (Djwal Khul & Hilarion- Emerald Green/Pale Green) helps you find the right place and the right time. Bottle # 60 (Lao Tsu & Kwan Yin- Blue/Clear) brings peace and acceptance of what life places in our path.

Dear Sarah
How did I end up like this? My partner and I moved to Ireland from Wales three years ago with our daughter. We all live in a bed-sit type flat, and are waiting to hear about a council property. We have had difficult health problems too. Can you offer any guidance?

Have you noticed how everything has gone wrong for you since you moved to Ireland? I strongly feel it is not the right place for you. I think you should imagine what your father's advice might be, and act on it. It is important that you go home.

You mention family rows and stress, and with your accommodation situation this is not surprising. If you follow this guidance there is a good job offer for your partner back in the United Kingdom. Do you have relations in London?

I feel that life would turn around for you if you check out housing in the leafy suburbs of the south. Surbiton might sound rather banal, but the schools would be good, and you would feel more supported with new friends.

I can see that you love the Welsh hills and valleys, but I think one of your reasons in moving to Ireland was the promise of pastures new. It has not really worked has it? You would find London stimulating and more hospitable than your present environment. Also, you will be able to do more world travel for family holidays – Spain and Greece. There is definitely a much better lifestyle awaiting you.

You have a good relationship with your partner, and he is committed to you. It would be a shame to put the family through too much more torture. I even think that everyone's health will improve in a more conducive living environment.

You have been caught with accidents and pregnancies and it is a good testimony to your relationship that you have stayed together. I think you need to decide on a plan of action and get yourselves out of here.

Your partner will probably be in two minds about the idea – anything for an easy life. However, once you have made the move there is no looking back. He needs to check out work contacts in the UK. The building trade seems to be a good way back to decent money.

I visualise your daughter very happy in an old primary school. She would certainly be a lot easier if you had more space. You could decide to stay, in which case I would envisage a continuation of the struggle. So, it is time to take the bull by the horns. Try to make your move as soon as you can. Good Luck!

Subject: How People Change

Aura Soma Bottle # 3 (Atlantean Bottle- Blue/Green) supports the heart with life's ebb and flow. Bottle # 75 (Go with the Flow- Magenta/Turquoise) helps you to accept life's changing pattern.

Dear Sarah
I have just been inexplicably dumped by a long term friend. The last time we met everything was normal between us. I am really confused and feel paranoid. Should I be worried about my future?

You have heard the expression "there's nowt as strange as folk?" Really there is never a simple explanation when a friend or lover dumps you after a long time. But if you think over it carefully, you will realise that change has been in the air for quite a while.

It is a fact of life that people develop and grow apart. There is never a straightforward reason for this. The Chinese I-Ching philosophy describes life's inevitable flux very well. There is an unwritten law of the Universe that change is constant. Whether it is dramatic or measured, nothing stays the same. This is the nature of our reality and we make a big mistake if we expect life to remain stagnant. It is inevitable that neither our happiness nor our misery will be maintained. This is encouraging when we are in the doldrums but unnerving when we are happy with our lot.

Our unconscious knows the importance of dynamic shifts and senses events long before we accept them in our conscious mind. The mixed blessing of being able to foretell the future reflects this. If we know things in advance we run the risk of moving ahead of ourselves. Everything gets turned upside down and our destiny gets potentially scrambled. I have met people who dug deep holes for themselves because they trusted a stranger's predictions. To take things as they come and to listen to our selves offers the best way forward. We then resist the temptation to prejudge, act prematurely, or come unstuck.

Take life's changes in your stride, and accept that they are part of its rich tapestry. We would find things dull if they always remained the same; and that includes our happy states. Like children with too many presents we would soon mess with the rubbish, if things went too much our way. Too often we walk around in the pursuit of happiness not realising that is the challenges of life that confirm our reality. Change is both logical and desirable, so go with the flow and embrace everything, even the unsettling and disturbing experiences.

Philosophy lesson over: back to your friend. She has been quite rude in offering you no explanation for her behaviour. This is a way for her to retain control. To keep you guessing means she still has the Ace up her sleeve. My advice is walk away. What kind of friend dumps you with no explanation? It stings and it hurts, but if someone is not for you be wary.

People have very odd agendas. Only be interested in unconditional love and acceptance. If someone is short-changing you, or a situation is unequal; leave it behind. True, we are all human, and there is always scope for forgiveness. But I would not play into this person's hands or get wound up by the situation. Your 'friend' does not understand herself, so she can offer you no reason. She has gone quiet to get perspective and recharge her batteries.

An apology would be courteous, but also rather inadequate. Move on and let her wonder about you in time. As she loses her grip on your life, she will miss you and re-contact you. At which point you may feel so annoyed you tell her where to go. The dynamic has changed between you. You no longer serve her ego or purpose, so your usefulness has played out. Ask yourself, was she ever really a friend?

Subject: **Work Attraction**

Aura Soma Bottle # 47 (Old Soul Bottle- Royal Blue/Lemon) helps process karmic situations that get a grip of your mind and heart. Bottle # 87 (The Wisdom of Love- Coral/Coral) supports suffering inspired by unrequited love.

Dear Sarah
I'm finding it difficult to forget someone I met at work. They cast a spell on me and used me to their advantage. I have genuine feelings for this person but when they left work they refused to keep in touch. I feel so used.

Deep connections at work are very common. People have a natural link and share the same environment. The working conditions will unify some relationships and sabotage others. You have been the victim of someone who took advantage of your good nature and used you to gain control socially. Because of your deep feelings you were susceptible to their manipulation. You were not able to distance yourself and so objectify the situation.

I feel sorry for you. It is a harsh fact of life that there are people at large who need to play out power issues at the expense of more trusting souls. Often such a person is deeply insecure. They need to reassure themselves that they are desirable, powerful and smart. When they find someone they can use to good effect they will be unscrupulous. This behaviour indicates a calculating, devious and manipulative personality who believes that life must revolve around "number one."

Your reality check came when they cut you off because you were no longer useful. A deep part of you cannot believe they have switched behaviour so quickly. At one time all over you like a rash, this person has moved on without a second thought. It is time to wake up! There is no excuse for those lies, which were a feeble attempt to see if they could break up your relationship. I would recommend that you move forward fairly lively, or they just might succeed in their mission.

Make sure you have your priorities right. It could be that you are in love with this player, in which case I almost pity you. It would be a great shame to throw in the towel with your long-term partner, particularly for someone who does not really love you. You knew all along that they were spoken for and no doubt the flirting was fun at times. However there are now more serious issues at stake. At work you made each other's lives more comfortable, but do remember that the dynamic has changed. Where are they?

Try to put this episode behind you for the moment. There is an irony to this story. When this person's marriage fails they will do a U-turn and experience a lot of remorse. Do remember that you have not seen the last of them. This situation could actually have quite serious long-term repercussions. Your own partner is not oblivious to the feelings you are carrying for someone else. I am surprised by their composure. This would indicate that deeper issues are playing out. It is natural that other attractions happen – it is a fact of life. What you do about them is the key to how this ends. You have some soul searching to do. I do not believe this manipulator will make you happy, but sure it is your life.

Just remember the grass is not always greener, and if you decide to leave your current relationship there is a high likelihood that you will repent at leisure. I know that you are not going to take my word for it, so I wish you the best –some things are meant to be!

Subject: **Kiss And Tell?**

Aura Soma Bottle # 40 ('I Am'- Red/Gold) will free you up from old, limiting patterns. Bottle # 24 (New Message- Violet/Turquoise) helps you to connect with your Soul Mate.

Dear Sarah
I had quite an intense emotional connection with a famous person for a stretch of time. Recently he is ignoring me and acting as if I don't exist. I am so tempted to sell my story. What should I do?

Difficult this. On one hand the woman scorned is a dangerous creature indeed. But on the other you have to consider your reputation, and the privacy of your family and friends. In many respects you do not owe this person anything. But you are essentially loyal, even though spurned. The temptation to kick up a bit is quite strong, but what will you achieve by this? So far you have acted with discretion and integrity. Why stop now? Be careful in this situation. You probably still love this person and are reacting because you are hurt. It is very important that you think carefully before you act in haste and repent at leisure. Do you really want to be tabloid fodder for a week or so? I think that you know you deserve more than this.

Hold onto your hat is what I say. Things are not as they seem around your heart's desire. A storm is a brewing, and if you do not want to be caught up in a mess, I suggest you exit left, rather quickly. You have every reason to be proud of yourself. Despite your strong feelings you did not respond directly to this man's advances.

Top marks for respecting his position and status. His complete denial of previous actions is however very difficult to cope with. The way that he has buried his head in the sand will only work for so long. Mr Ostrich has to do what he has to do.

Really you are better off accepting the way things are. They have come to this point for a very good reason. You have supported and helped this man in a lot of ways. This has strengthened his resolve to honour his commitments. Why now undo everything you helped to honour? Move on with your dignity intact remembering that men hail from planet Zog. Well, a lot of them do.

Be aware that it is an inherent male tendency, to keep all options open. The male species is expert at keeping something simmering in the background "just in case." I'm afraid you have allowed yourself to get caught up in just such a scenario.

Love is blind, and you have certainly been patient, if not a little misguided. He chose you carefully in a way, knowing that your integrity would protect the situation. You provided a safe and reassuring background presence. I know this does not help the fact that you invested a lot in this man in every sense.

Please do not feel you have wasted many years and precious time. You did what you did. Do not forget, the show is not over, until the fat lady sings; and she has not so much as cleared her throat yet.

For your own sake, move on and do not do anything stupid. The karma and balance of this triangle will continue to play out in interesting ways. The test is what you do with it.

Plenty of people would point the finger and not understand if you talk anyway, so there is another good reason to keep quiet. You certainly do not want to subject yourself to endless explanations or recrimination.

Hold onto what you know and keep your secrets. Life has a way of turning things around. You will reap your reward in other ways.

Subject: **Moral Dilemma**

Aura Soma Bottle # 18 (Turning Tide- Yellow/Violet) helps a person adjust to change on a deep level, which has its roots in the deep distant past.

Dear Sarah
I feel tortured. I think that I love someone other than my wife of 16 years. What should I do? I consider myself moral and I do not want to hurt anyone. Help!

Morality is a strange concept. What is Okay for one person may be beyond contempt for another. It is all relative, and depends to what extent we justify an action. Whatever our morals I think most people would agree that it is a sin to be untrue to ourselves. That is dishonest. At least if we come clean people can come to terms with our decisions. What is wrong is to live with the distress of emotional limbo. Of course we all do this times, but it is when the situation becomes persistently unbearable that we should act.

In terms of the wedding vows, eloping with someone other than your wife is questionable. However, the church now recognises that forgiveness and release can be more important than staying in a marriage which is beyond repair. Every case is different and it is a personal choice when to quit. I don't think there is any justification for honouring a relationship that is physically or emotionally destructive.

The energy drain of such unions is wrong. What is more difficult to discern is whether a slippers and sofas marriage is valid. Is it undermining or comforting? Is a relationship that has become largely platonic a legitimate basis for marriage? Plenty of people would settle for this on the grounds that familiarity provides a kind of security.

Family commitments often defer any soul searching, and prevent precipitous behaviour. However, once the slow erosion of complacency threatens the Status Quo, it is time to get radical. This does not inevitably mean the end of a marriage, but it does signify a shake-up – A "shape up or ship out" moment.

I would certainly not encourage you to betray your wife for the sake of a lustful attraction. But, it seems as if you have actually outgrown your partner and fallen in love with someone else.

Resisting temptation is admirable, but there is a danger that true passion will come up and bite us between the eyes despite ourselves. Mutual love for the children is all that some people need to stay together, for others family ties produce a bleak and frustrating existence. If you learn to distinguish love from the 'in love' feeling, decisions are easier. The in love flutter will disappear if you ignore it. True love will grow despite your efforts to be good.

Only time will verify the sanctity of your new emotions. It is not a crime to fall in love, but once you are sure of your feelings it is better to honour them. Do not stay in the comfort zone for the sake of it. Love has a way of finding a path through a maze of complexity.

Subject: **Paternity Suit?**

Aura Soma Bottle # 50 (El Morya- Pale Blue/Pale Blue) helps a person discern Divine will in a complex situation.

Dear Sarah
I am wrestling with my conscience and don't know what to do. I am unsure of the paternity of my child. Do I tell my child and the father of the doubt or do I keep quiet? I no longer have a full relationship with the man concerned. But I am worried about the moral aspect of my child knowing who her father is.

Medical research shows how commonplace your dilemma is. A large percentage of fathers have questions about the true paternity of at least one of their children. Although it is traditional for young lads to shirk their responsibility when a child is conceived "It can't be mine. I wasn't there," is the usual protestation. But, it must be every grown man's nightmare, to be told that a child he has raised and loves was not his in the first place.

Sociological questions about the *definition* of paternity help in these cases. Admittedly the biological father is not *inevitably* the man who nurtures and provides for the children. So who then is the *real* father? It is a harsh fact of life that relationships break down and affairs happen. We live in complicated times, but then has not human nature always has been complex?

There are no easy answers to your question. What is the moral solution? Secrets like this can be carried to the grave. But on the other hand they can be exposed at the most unexpected times. It must be very stressful living with the knowledge that you are possibly pulling the wool over the eyes of the acting father, the *real* father and your child. This of course brings us to DNA testing. Logically this can be sorted out fairly quickly. The paternity of a child can be established by blood tests of the parties involved. But the important question is do you really want to face up to the truth, or continue to live what is potentially a lie? You are right eye colouring is a significant indicator of paternity. Particularly rare is a brown-eyed child from two blue-eyed parents; rare but apparently not completely impossible.

The real issues run deeper than the colouring or complexion of your child. Why do you not want to find out the truth for sure? What aspects of your self will not let this man go? You did pin the paternity on him when you knew he probably was not biologically responsible.

Do be aware that in time, your very sensitive child may be in a biology class and realise that something simply does not add up. Your child already has an in-built instinctive connection to the probable father. Nature does not lie. So what you hold back at this point will probably resurface in years to come. Hopefully then everyone would be able to cope with the truth. But if you keep quiet now you are risking great recriminations from everyone concerned in time. Can you live with the pressure of this deception?

The resemblance of your child to the *other* man is undeniable. You are running the show at the moment by denying the awkward truth and innocent people are being misled.

It could be that everyone has an unspoken knowledge of the truth. The unconscious has an uncanny way of knowing and working things out. There is an undefined unease, and energies usually find a way to the fore when something needs to be addressed. In a way I feel this is the case. You are caught up in a hugely loaded karmic scenario. So, as long as the equilibrium is maintained and everyone is happy to play out the role assigned. All power to you. Be aware however, that the truth will out. I believe your child will work it out for themselves.

How strongly do you feel; and how resolved are you to carry this burden? Unravelling the truth now would be messy, but can you cope with the alternative? I can only recommend honesty. Listen to your instincts, and let the rest follow.

Subject: **Volatile Wife**

Aura Soma Bottle # 28 (Maid Marion- Green/Red) assists a male will that hen pecked feeling. Bottle # 10 (Go Hug a Tree- Green/Green) will bring a sense of personal space however claustrophobic the situation.

Dear Sarah
My wife is so volatile that mountains are made out of molehills, and over the past ten years she has frequently left our home. The cat, dog and her family all come before me. She says it is always my fault yet I try to be the peacemaker. What is going on with her?

I think you have shown your wife remarkable patience and tolerance. How about "no more Mr Nice Guy?" She is really taking advantage of your good nature. I think it is time to make it clear that you will not put up with her irrational behaviour any longer. You are a victim in this situation. She has walked all over you and has manipulated you financially and emotionally. I feel that she has deliberately manoeuvred her marriages for monetary gain. She is sharp and cute. It is very important for her to know that she is materially secure, and she is not focused upon love at all. Her emotional issues are of course suppressed by drink, and she has almost become deadened to this aspect of her life. She is hard to reach because she has forgotten who she is. Really she is battling for survival because she feels life is cruel. She does not realise that you are there waiting to connect. She is afraid to love, as she believes everyone she loves will leave her. This becomes a self-fulfilling prophecy as she behaves in ways that push love away.

I am afraid that you are fighting a losing battle. You are competing with the drink at this stage, and really she needs to help herself. Letting her go might be the healthiest way to achieve the shift that you both need. As you say she is requesting a divorce, and to be honest I feel that you would be mad to contest it. I think you are aware of this. There are many monsters in her head that she should confront. Unfortunately I do not feel she will get round to conquering them in this life, so do yourself a favour and cut loose.

The best thing you could do would be to get a different perspective. Make the most of your connections abroad. Australia looks like a very positive place for you to at least visit. Please do not feel a failure when this marriage ends. You really have done your best against terrible odds. There is no point trying to change your wife. She is dealing with a lot of hidden anger, and suppressed rage that has nothing to do with you. The most loving thing you could do would be to give up. Surrender the situation to the universe, and trust that you will be delivered. You deserve better than this.

Subject: **Lack Of Fulfilment**

Aura Soma Bottle #85 (Titania- Turquoise/Clear) helps remove creative blockages and assists the communication of the heart. This bottle encourages the expression of suppressed feelings.

Dear Sarah
I am at my wits end. I have been married now for 12 years. I love my husband to bits and I know he loves me, because if he didn't he would be gone long ago. Can you tell me anything that will give me hope for the future? The only thing keeping me going is the fact I have work full time outside the home.

I know that you believe the gap in your life is the lack of a baby, but really this is quite a dangerous way to think. You so desperately want another child and yet you are referring to your son as the product of a 'previous mistake'! It is as if you resent him and have a problem accepting his existence. Your husband clearly does love you. He married you and accepted another man's child. It would be a shame to jeopardise all the good things in your life by fixating on the "if onlys." You are lucky to have a loving husband, a full time job and a son, who incidentally looks as if he is in line to win the lotto by his nineteenth birthday.

Count your blessings and relax. You must know that it is not a good idea to bring a baby into a stressed environment. And it is certainly not a good idea to believe that everything will be ok once another baby comes along. For a start you would be tied to the house for a while; an idea that you seem to resent. Also, babies should never be viewed as the glue that keeps a relationship together.

Mother's the world over will tell you that if a relationship is not strong a baby stretches things to breaking point. Have you actually thought about what the reality of a baby in your life would mean? Perhaps the universe is protecting you from yourself at this point.

The doctors are right there is nothing apparently wrong with you. However, a deep part of your psyche is rejecting a baby. You value your own space. You have still not processed the hurt of your previous mistake, and you are looking for a sign of hope. This could be a case of getting what you need rather than what you think you want. We all carry beliefs that our lives would be complete if only such and such happened. What we are not listening to is the rumblings of our own power deep within. All of us have a strong capacity to make things happen that we either do not recognise or are afraid of. This is the time for you to move up a notch and become more spiritually aware.

You are being challenged to find out that there are other non-visible dimensions to your life. There is an internal pilgrimage on the cards for you. You can choose to run away from this and continue to resent life. Or you can accept the beauty of every present moment and move beyond feeling stuck. I believe that you will be a mum again but that you will be quite a different person when this happens.

Tai chi would be a brilliant way for you to connect with your life force. There are ways to address the blocks in your life energetically and you will find these. Trust that you will be shown the way forward. If you can find a piece of moonstone jewellery to wear you will find balance hormonally. You will also find it very supportive to all the issues arising from being a woman and a mum. The ease with which you glide through life will be tangible.

CHAPTER NINE:
Career

Subject: **Own Business?**

Aura Soma Bottle # 19 (Living in the Material World- Red/Purple) supports those who have financial survival issues.

Dear Sarah
I am fascinated how you can tell so much about someone from a letter. How is it possible to help people you have never even met? Also I have put a lot of effort into my business pioneering an 'alternative' product. Will it pay off?

Believe it or not it is possible to send healing energy to someone even though we are not in their company. We all do this every time we pray. Of course nothing beats prayer, but there are also visualisation techniques that may increase your effectiveness. This does not mean that creative power allows us to manipulate things to our liking. Divine will usually has a more measured agenda, which may pass us by if we are too fixated on manifesting our heart's desire. There are serious lessons to be learned for those who attempt to step beyond the loving confines of God's will. Frequently people are attracted to the spiritual path by the concept of abundance, believing that adhering to certain disciplines will bring riches. This invariably gets blocked. Many of us are still living out deeply ingrained vows of poverty that equate money and material goods with evil. So cut those ties, and believe that you are entitled to abundance on all levels by the grace of God.

Sometimes we try too hard to make a success of things, when what the universe requires is simple trust. Your angels are available to you at all times, so ask them for help. But do not forget your own responsibility to yourself. God helps those who help themselves.

Always remain grounded and reserve your judgement, particularly with finances. It is a mistake that a lot of people make. Just because a business is loosely based around the alternative trappings of spirituality, its success is not guaranteed. The spirit world may have a completely different plan for you. These lessons are about remaining open and surrendering our little will (ego) to the greater will (God).

Trying to trick the angels into what we believe to be our divine right does not wash. They work for our better good at all times so don't be conned by false promises. You will make greater strides if you hand your project over. Give up trying so hard and ask your guides if this is really what you are meant to be doing. Remember things are never quite as they seem: it was Cinderella who went to the ball and landed Prince Charming!

Subject: **Career And Multiple Sclerosis**

Aura Soma Bottle # 25 (Florence Nightingale- Purple/Magenta) is supportive of those with ME. It assists mobility and convalescence. Bottle # 47 (Old Soul- Royal Blue/Lemon) will support the damaged nerve endings of the MS condition.

Dear Sarah

I am staring a business venture with a friend of mine. Will it be a success? Also, my boyfriend has recently been diagnosed with MS – he is finding it difficult to adjust. Do you see any light at the end of the tunnel for him?

Your business stands to be a great success. I see you travelling regularly to develop your contacts abroad. You need to do the correct groundwork, and make sure that the contracts and business plan are sound. In particular, you have good business acumen. You are more creative and tenacious than your prospective partner. She brings different gifts to the company. She would be very capable on the administrative side, and will do a lot of the laborious tasks to great effect. You will eventually strike out on your own, but for the moment it is wise to go with the plan.

Your boyfriend is facing a huge challenge. He is someone who likes to know where he stands, and he always tries to map out the way ahead.

The uncertainty of the progression of this illness will be causing him a lot of stress. It is best to encourage him to live in the present moment. If he can handle his mental reactions he has a high chance of keeping his illness at bay.

Buy him a piece of Turquoise, a powerful healing stone which supports people with conditions like this.

There are three minerals called Williamsite, Valencianite and Chrysotile, which have a high success rate with MS. It is a good idea for him to avoid refined and sweet foods. Finally, the Aura Soma bottle Turning Tide, is very useful for letting go of the fear associated with degenerative illness: it enables the healing to kick in. By the age of thirty, he will have made major adjustments successfully. I think you will marry in the next couple of years, and have at least two children. Healing can create miracles in this situation, so never underestimate what can happen. Anything is possible.

Subject: **What Is Next?**

Aura Soma Bottle # 58 (Orion and Angelica- Pale Blue/Pale Pink) helps inner and outer travel and helps to clarify your direction.

Dear Sarah
I'm restless! I have been living in Ireland for two years. I've done quite well for myself, but want to travel, and see if there is more for me elsewhere.

Your hunch is correct. You have gone as far as you can here. I can see that you have an enjoyable social life, and that you are well liked. However months of working anti-social hours, and a failed relationship have taken their toll. You have a brother who lives in the Far East, and you have saved enough money to travel. I really think you should join him. There is a connection in Australia that you must make the most of, and Thailand is very significant on a spiritual level. Like your grandfather, and your brother you are destined to meet your partner abroad. By the age of twenty-six you will be settled and happy. You will have a wonderful family life, and I am certain that Edinburgh would suit you as a place to live in the future. Work is plentiful during your travels, and you get more out of a place when you experience it over a number of months. Your cards indicate that you will weigh these issues up carefully and leave by October.

Subject: **Russian Orthodox**

Aura Soma Bottle # 77 (The Cup- Clear/Magenta) helps you let go of your illusions and see clearly. It reveals the true quality of a person. Bottle # 24 (New Message- Violet/Turquoise) attracts your soul mate.

Dear Sarah
Hi, I'm a Russian girl who has lived in Ireland for some time. I'm Christian Orthodox, I believe in God and Love. My problem is my private life and happiness. I really want to create a family and have children. Will I find a husband? I'm planning to work on cruise ships. Is it good for me and will it happen?

I can appreciate that you are very connected with the Russian man you are seeing. But as you know he is not free. Your relationship works in the context of this country and you are clearly a mutual support for each other. He is actually quite strict with himself on moral issues, but he has found you irresistible. There is definitely a soul mate bond between you. I believe that he was your father in a previous existence. If you consider the security and comfort that he brings I think you will identify this link. But just as daughters must grow and develop away from home, so you must spread your wings. We both know that this man will not abandon his wife and son. You must take a leap of faith and see how you get on without him. Really the offer of work abroad is what is needed to break free. You should give yourself a few months apart.

Do not end the connection completely. Simply tell him you want to travel and save money for a few months. I see a very tempting work offer coming in which you should accept. Work on a cruise ship will give you the space you need to get a perspective on your life. You have more independence and personal power than you appreciate. This is what you must tap into. In a sense you do not need a man around, and when you appreciate this, a wonderful relationship will manifest. I do see a third marriage for you that will be much more lasting and successful than your previous two. I think that you should stay friends with this man. I do not think it is necessary to have an abrupt parting.

You certainly do love each other, but sometimes part of love is recognising the right time to let go. Really, if he is worthwhile as a continuing influence in your life, he will accept the importance of this trip. I am particularly drawn to the Caribbean. The atmosphere of the Grenadines will suit you; Saint Lucia, and Barbados especially. You will find peace of mind if you step forward at this point. If you do not your situation will continue to cause you unease. There are great friends and contacts waiting on board, so focus on the new excitements. Before you know it you will be wondering why you stayed in Ireland for so long.

CHAPTER TEN:
Spiritual Landscape

Subject: **Name Changing**

Aura Soma Bottle # 81 (Unconditional Love- Pink/Pink) will help you to love yourself just the way you are. It also offers a new beginning for love.

Dear Sarah
I have never liked my name. I feel that my life could be different with a change of name. I was waiting until I married but there is no sign of a relationship. Would a name change sort my life out?

You are right in one respect, changing your name can alter the energetic frequency of your life. But it is not something to undertake lightly. If you have never been comfortable with your full name then a trip to the deed pole office certainly makes sense. But make sure you choose something that is truly you. I have met people who have made drastic changes to their name and there is a peculiar phoniness about them. It is as if they have studied 101 books on numerology, and contrived a recipe that will reel in every good thing. The names of such people certainly add up to wonderful possibilities. But often they have plucked something out of the air that does not resonate with their energies.

There is something to be said for holding onto the name your mother gives you at birth: she is the person most in tune with you. She has borne you and birthed you. So be careful who you marry, or retain your maiden name if you feel it brings you luck.

Letters correspond to numbers, and in combination the spelling of a name can up add to a powerful energy. Linda Goodman's book *Star Signs* is an excellent book on numerology. She presents the Chaldean-Hebrew numerical alphabet, which is the truest and oldest numbers system. Have fun playing about with the possibilities, but often the simpler the change you make the better.

For example with the name Sarah: if I drop the "h" I suddenly turn from the victim energy of a no 12, to the spiritual energy of a no 7. You may ask why I have not done so. It is a long story, but the upshot is, the combination of my full name Sarah Delamere Hurding suits me just fine. It creates numerically the master number 33 so that is a great energy.

For bringing a relationship into your life, there are less drastic and equally effective ways to a name change. Usually blocks to romance start in the bedroom, so get decorating and de-clutter this most important place. Also revamp your appearance. Spend time on yourself so that you feel content with who you are.

Worthwhile relationships arrive generally when you are zooming around on your own not giving men a second thought. Do change your name if it makes sense for you to do so. But make sure this is done legally and that all documents carry your new frequency. Take time to sit with any such change and be certain that it resonates with who you truly are. The outside world has to agree with you for the magic to take effect.

Subject: **Is Psychic Work Against God's will?**

Aura Soma Bottle # 86 (Oberon- Clear/Turquoise) helps communication for the light. Bottle # 83 (Open Sesame- Turquoise/Gold) opens the door for new insight on ancient truths. Bottle # 5(The Sunset bottle- Yellow/Red) supports those who have been abused.

Dear Sarah
The work you are doing is against God. The bible condemns people like you. Read the gospel of John and repent. What gives you the right to advise a wife to leave her husband? Some spiritual healer!

As you can see my mailbag this week has been interesting. So I will exercise my own right to reply. Firstly Sir, you have judged me too quickly. I am in fact a committed Christian. Admittedly I am working in a very controversial way, but do not forget that Christ himself broke all the boundaries. The spirit of the gospel is meant to shake you up and rattle your cage. The light can break through into the world in the most unexpected ways, and it does not always happen in a church.

I do admittedly walk a spiritual tightrope with this work, but we all do. Every day should be a careful one, even for those who happily attend Sunday services. There is never any room for spiritual complacency, and sometimes in the middle of a contradiction is the place to be. So you look after your faith, and I will continue to monitor mine.

Christ said "he who is without sin throw the first stone" We can all be too quick to pass judgement. It is a failing of the flesh that makes us feel better about our own convictions. So do not jump too quickly: things are not always as they seem. Incidentally John the Baptist was a great prophet and seer. Being from a Pentecostal church, you will also know that one of the gifts of the Spirit is the gift of prophecy. If my work sends people running back to the churches I would be the first to say "yippee!"

The letter you refer to was written for a woman who had suffered a lifetime of physical and mental abuse from her husband. Do you really feel it would have been responsible for me to advise her to stay put? Again what I wrote pushed a few buttons. I would always honour a marriage and family life, and fully respect people who have made those sacraments. However, sometimes the most healing way forward for families that suffer is the freedom to move on.

It is never right for people to experience abuse a moment longer than they have to. Separation does not mean that families never communicate again, but it does break rights of ownership and control where these dominate family life.

So all the best to my critics. I am delighted to see that such controversial issues are stirring up your own beliefs. Do make sure however that you fully understand something before you throw stones. Incidentally, at some point if the correct funding comes along, I will soon be opening an international healing and study centre where such topics religious and social will be addressed. The world needs such places, following all the scandals within the church, and particularly because of the surge of interest in the New Age. It will be a Christian centre, but all cynics, sceptics, and alternative believers would be welcome.

Subject: **Political Deception**

Aura Soma Bottle # 90 (Wisdom Rescue- Gold/Deep Magenta) helps order to arise from chaos.

Dear Sarah
Since the Twin Towers accident I have been having nightmares. The publicity surrounding Sellafield at the moment is making me even more worried. Are we all doomed? My recurring dream is that I am trapped at the top of a blazing tower. I know I can fly to escape but I don't I wake up just at the point when I jump.

There is a lot of scare mongering in the public consciousness at the moment. Certain people are plucking issues from the air to further their own purpose. But what is new? Politicians have always manipulated the media in order to justify both their policies and their actions.

At the time of writing, Bush and Blair between them are about to convince us that action against Iraq is a good idea. Of course the need to address the terrorist threat is obvious since the Twin Towers disaster, but there is a danger in anticipating what may be next.

I have said this many times but we draw our greatest fears towards us if we give them too much airtime. Our mind is a powerful creative instrument, which has the capacity to manifest what we expect given enough time. I do not need to remind you of the Hollywood movies, and video games that anticipated the Twin Towers nightmare. Now the question is did the energy of that creative imagination attract the disaster or did it simply prophesy the event?

In my opinion it is the different energies at play that we need to be aware of in the political arena. Many disasters are drawn onto the earth because we expect them. I do not mean to be irresponsible whilst making these points but we can turn things around with a different approach. For example it is clear that the Toxic Sellafield plant is not doing the environment any favours. But what are we doing when we anticipate a Chernobyl type disaster for Ireland?

Unfortunately, nuclear power is a reality in modern society and Sellafield, whilst not exactly safe is more of a threat to the UK than to Ireland. I certainly do not foresee a terrorist attack upon Sellafield, unless of course we go on about it so much that they oblige us. My feeling is that politically we are being hoodwinked. Whilst Bush has the potential to sort out a major terrorist threat, he also has the worrying ability to aggravate and upset the delicate infrastructure of the Middle East. Sure this is already happening and there is not much we can do about it. There are plenty of destructive energies at play in the world at the moment and planetary healing was never more needed. Do not be alarmed, as there are many people who understand energies working behind the scenes to help us all. The more conscious and awake we all become the better, so do not live in fear but work to develop your own creative energy. The more positive and energetically responsible we are the more chance we have of survival.

Subject: **Catholicism And Readings**

Aura Soma Bottle # 49 (New Messenger- Turquoise/Violet) helps you discern your true spiritual path. It resolves old guilt feelings and assists discrimination.

Dear Sarah
I was brought up a Catholic. I am curious but nervous about psychic readings. Are they sinful? Are they truthful?

Firstly, if you have any doubts about something that might threaten your spiritual integrity, do not engage with it. There is a melting pot of pseudo spirituality for sale. Faith is precious, truth is important, and hope is a fundamental necessity. There is no point in courting guidance that delivers a semblance of plausibility, and then twists the outcome in a rather sinister way. In the bible there are plenty of warnings against false prophecy.

Jeremiah tells us to watch out for people who "speak visions from their own minds," and John commands us to "test the spirits to see whether they are from God."

There is no doubt that some people are gifted with profound imagination, and the ability to receive messages from, what Carl Jung called, the universal unconscious. However, how do we know what they are tapping into? It is important to take the message on board but reserve judgement. Something claiming to be prophetic may be a lie designed to mislead you. Do not forget there are mischievous spirits that try to have fun at our expense.

In Corinthians, Paul names prophesy as one of the most desirable gifts of the spirit. In the right context prophecy can be healing, encouraging, and positive. With wisdom and discernment there is a place for giving people hope.

As I have implied, there can be a huge gap between psychic ability and spirituality. They do not necessarily travel hand in hand. Just as a psychic can be operating without an ounce of compassion, leaving a trail of disaster, so can a priest be self-serving and corrupt. Just as a priest can be genuine and concerned, so can a psychic of integrity provide a service that brings peace and reassurance. God moves in mysterious ways.

A lot of our curiosity about the future is akin to the folly of the Garden of Eden. We are fascinated by the power of knowing and perhaps we feel it gives us more control over our lives. Although it is possible to look into the energies that are shaping our future, it is not always wise to do so. True spirituality reveres simplicity, and it is good to develop contentment with the present moment of our everyday lives. Grace is certainly the most powerful energy we can ally ourselves to.

Subject: **Personal Development**

Aura Soma Bottle # 43 (Creativity- Turquoise/Turquoise) helps you connect with your creativity minus complications. Bottle # 23 (Love and Light- Rose Pink/Pink) helps you find inner and outer harmony.

Dear Sarah
I am writing to you because I feel torn between success and failure. Reiki has helped me in the last 12 months to grow and develop. But on the other hand my family life is a shambles. I feel torn between my personal growth and my unhappiness towards my husband and my children.

By taking Reiki attunements you have opened yourself to the abundance of the universe. Such a change to your energies is not always an easy adjustment. Because your own perspectives are undergoing a process of purification you are more sensitised to the chaos around you. A word of warning: it is possible to get a bit precious about negativity. Of course be careful about protecting your energetic space, but there is no need to prune your life too drastically. We still have to live in the real world.

In your letter you are clearly weighing up the legitimacy of your family life, as if to some extent you have now outgrown it. This of course may be the case. Time will tell. Reiki certainly does have the tendency to chop the dead wood from our lives. But there is no need to force change ourselves, especially not on behalf of the people we live with. If anything you should now be more tolerant and compassionate to those around you.

There is no need to beat yourself up to the extent that you do. I feel you are unnecessarily hard on yourself. Are you sure your family are deliberately making you feel guilty about spending time on yourself? I think you might be projecting this onto them. Everyone is entitled to do their own thing; even mums deserve some space and respect.

Underneath it all I feel that you need to be needed, and that you have certain expectations of your husband and children. None of them are towing the line, and they are all proving difficult in their own sweet way. What you have to do is to allow them the space to express themselves in whatever way they choose. That way their rebellions should cease. Each of them is trying to make their subversive impact on the situation. As soon as they realise the strict boundaries have gone they will automatically be responsible on their own terms.

Do your own thing in an independent and guilt freeway, and let everyone else do the same. Giving up control in this way is very difficult. But if you trust the powers that be, to take care of your loved ones you will be delighted at the long-term results.

Reiki allows you to heal the people around you as well as yourself. So send some positive energy to your family and accept the results. This is important. We should not try to manipulate people to perform in a way that suits our own agenda. Surrender your hopes and dreams and have more belief in destiny. Que Sera Sera!

Subject: **Corrupt Priest**

Aura Soma Bottle # 16 (The Violet Robe- Violet/Violet) helps someone awaken to their true self. Bottle # 56 (St. Germain- Pale Violet/Pale Violet) releases negativity on all levels.

Dear Sarah
After my birth in the 30's our Parish Priest called to my mother and told her that one day I would be the only one left. He also told me that I would never have happiness in this life and that a curse was following our family. What is the curse and who put it on us? Please help me.

Oh please. Did you never think to question the authority of this priest? What right did he have to instil fear in your mind? Even if the existence of a curse were true, I think your priest was highly irresponsible to tell you. Why did he not offer you prayer and protection instead of trying to impress you with a sense of black wonder? This *man* has been a very negative influence on your psyche, never mind the alleged curse.

The intrinsic power of a curse is the belief that it is there and that it can floor you. It is possible to reverse the sentence by sending it back to the original person: with love. You do not even have to know the identity of the sender to do this. Just light a candle, burn some frankincense and use a mirror to visualise the energy returned to sender.

Anyone who tampers with the dark energies should realise that what they are putting out will be returned to them threefold. This is a non-negotiable law of the universe. It is designed to surprise the ignorant, and warn the manipulative.

Having said that, we do inherit the sins of our fathers. This is a biblical idea, which is not meant to reduce us to a quivering wreck. Rather it should put us in awe of God and encourage us to turn to him for help. You have had a life of struggle and turmoil that was unfortunately part of your destiny. They do say that what does not destroy you will make you stronger. So I think you can give yourself the pat on the back that you deserve. You do not have to expect hardship any longer.

The message of the gospel is one of freedom. However difficult our lives if we have Christ on our side, we have the victory. Trust that the stronger powers of love and light surround you. There is no need to be afraid. Your family members did not pass on because of a curse. They went to the light at the appointed time. Nothing you could have said or done would have prevented this.

You have certainly had to cope with a lot of grief and trauma, but you also have the rest of your life to enjoy. The worst has already happened and you can gain strength from the fact that you can cope with anything. What you have weathered would have finished most of us off.

Just out of interest a few generations back there were two sisters in love with one of the men in your family. I believe he married the fairer of the two. The younger sister was very psychic and possibly cursed the marriage. I think there has been a knock on effect through the years. The family farm was prosperous at this time and the marriage was happy. Unfortunately I think the bad wish of the sister had a delayed reaction. It ends with you. You are free now to think of yourself. It is time to be selfish in the best possible way. There is a holiday coach trip that brings happiness and companionship. Enjoy yourself!

Subject: **Psychic Attack**

Aura Soma Bottle # 19 (Living in the Material World- Red/Purple) protects from the presence of unwanted entities and psychic attack.

Dear Sarah
I am frightened. Every time I meet a particular person disturbing things happen. I ignore my gut instinct about this person to be polite. But this week I have had so much bad luck its unreal. How can I protect myself?

Between the lines of your letter you are making a very serious but valid accusation. If you spelled everything out to a psychoanalyst they would take you in for a few days. Only kidding. I understand the challenge of this situation as in this line of work I have met many such experiences. Some healers and psychics prefer not to buy into the notion of psychic attack. But let me assure you it is very real and very dangerous.

The power of prayer is your main protection. The Bible talks about discernment of the spirits. This is crucial to remaining in one piece particularly if you are sensitive and open to different energies. A very important practical way to defend yourself is not to give these mischievous and reckless entities too much air time. But then we are back to those who choose to avoid the issue altogether. Which believe me if you are under attack is the last thing you can do.

So how do these attacks manifest? How can we protect ourselves if it happens? Firstly, avoid all activities which invite the nonsense in! Stay a mile away from Ouija boards, places and people that have a dark presence attached, and do not buy into this thing of doing spells to sort your life out.

I am horrified at the amount of books out there that encourage you to take on the manipulation of energy in order to get your own way. This is not to bad-mouth those who do good work and have integrity. However there is now a commercial tendency to sell everything; even the techniques of "playing God."

Unfortunately these tools, techniques and spells attract people who do not have an education in the dangers of energy. If you mess with such things you lay yourself wide open, you are throwing open the door to your soul. You can expect the consequences to be quite scary if you let in goodness only knows what. Go buy a Bible instead of a pack of cards?

These times are getting more dangerous; and the more interested we all get in things psychic, the more we are going to be tempted to meddle to find out what is there. Of course it is valid to ask questions and do research. Indeed education in these areas is very important. But please connect with people who have a good energy, a good heart and who are working with the light. This is where the discernment part is so important. Remember that Satan can manifest as an angel of light. Without getting too spooky here, just be careful out there.

If you are connected to the energy of crystals, you will find them a powerful tool of protection. Turquoise is very potent against the forces of darkness. The South Americans use it in their jewellery, for good reason. If you do healing or psychic work always make sure that the space you work in sacred and safe. You cannot be too careful, particularly now. The ignorance that seeks to discredit and sabotage good work is very prevalent. So if you are sound and bathed in angelic light expect to be challenged. Hang in there. Most importantly do not be afraid, as that feeds the darkness and such negativity may disable you.

This may sound quite potty to some readers. But I will take that risk. Having seen people have near-death experiences because of psychic attack, I want to make sure as many of you stay safe as possible. Just do not be overly paranoid about all this. Informed, balanced and protected is the way to be.

Subject: **Is Prediction Responsible?**

Aura Soma Bottle # 55 (The Christ- Clear/Red) gives a person the energy to follow their ideals.

Dear Sarah
How does prediction really help people to live responsibly? The Bible seems to warn against the quest for knowing the future. It emphasises the importance of daily trust in God. Where does Jesus fit in when you focus upon the intermedi-

ary nature of 'angels' and 'guides'? Surely predictive methods subvert the Christian tradition.

I agree in principle with all the points that you make in your letter. But I do not work in the same way as the fortune-teller you might find at the end of the pier. Primarily I am a healer who seeks to help those who ask for my perspective upon their problems. I do not see people who want a reading for entertainment or to satisfy their curiosity. I am a committed Christian who is admittedly working in a controversial way.

The church does not necessarily understand that there are many ways in which psychic insights can help people. Admittedly this work is spiritually dangerous. To be effective and accurate you have to have an awareness of energies and the possibilities of sabotage. There is no point in deceiving people or selling them lies which feed their fantasies. It all depends where you are coming from. The Bible says test the spirits and that is certainly something that I have to do a lot.

Exercising simple faith and daily trust in God is definitely preferable to zooming around the world's psychics trying to get the inside track on your future. It is better to keep life's mystery intact. However it is worth pointing out that the Bible is full of prophetic vision and that prophecy and its interpretation are amongst the gifts of the Spirit. Revelation is the Biblical term for prediction. This implies a spiritual consciousness that you will not necessarily find in a fortune-teller. However it is important not to tar everyone with the same brush.

There are amazing people of integrity who have gone "alternative" with their spirituality. So always reserve judgement and accept people as you find them.

In modern society we have to live with many options and much confusion. So really it is no wonder that people look for a little clarity. Psychic ability and alternative healing are not new. In fact they have been around longer than the established church and modern medical traditions.

Christ Consciousness is a strong feature of the New Age movement, though for the life of me I do not understand why they cannot drop the "conscious" bit. I think that once the appropriate bridges are built in the future it will be clear that what counts is spirituality and truth, not dogma. Oh dear that looks a bit like another prediction.

Subject: **Panic About Death**

Aura Soma Bottle # 2 (Peace Bottle- Blue/Blue) brings peace and enables you to look through the veil beyond this life and into the next world.

Dear Sarah
I am 26 years old and I seem to be very depressed and constantly worry about death. It is so bad that it wakes me up in the middle of the night and when I panic about it I can't seem to snap out of it! I don't want to be like this forever and wondered if you could help me somehow. I'm desperate.

There is peace of mind for you and it is not far away. All you have to do is reach out and take it. Call upon your Guardian Angel to take away the fear and believe it or not it will disappear. I will send you healing for this situation and if you could bring deep royal blue into your bedroom so much the better. I completely understand your predicament as I experienced the same thing for a number of years.

Your anxiety state indicates your sensitivity and your capacity for spiritual growth and healing. It is an energetic indication that you are very sensitive if not psychic. What may appear to others as a form of depression or neurosis is in fact a great gift that you can turn around to good effect. Strange as it may sound this, the most difficult time of your life will turn out to be the most powerful. You are waking up energetically and your sensitivity will enable you to heal people if you so choose.

I would recommend that you attend a Reiki master and receive an attunement in this energy. I can recommend someone to you if you contact me at the above number. This attunement allows your energy system to clear and detox over a twenty-one day span. You will find that it opens you up both spiritually and psychically but please make sure that you ask God for protection. Do not attend just anyone who claims to be able to help in this way. There are some strange energies at play, and it is important to be wise about what you get into. You do have the ability to heal in time but first you need to heal yourself.

Simply by writing your wish down in a letter you are expressing your determination to get through this trauma. Incidentally on a practical level Bach's Rescue Remedy is brilliant if you are feeling anxious. Yoga will also help you align your energies in a constructive way. You need this, not for the exercise but for the impact it will have upon your etheric and energetic system.

Not all depression has a clinical cause and there are many people who would benefit from an alternative approach to their problem rather than resort to pill popping. I have seen many clients be absolutely 100% better within themselves after just one healing session because the problem was not clinical but energetic. There are many types of depression and spiritually sensitive people respond well to healing. Do be assured that all will be well.

The fear of death is something we all have to look at sometimes. In your case it has become a preoccupation that you do not understand and want to be rid of. It does indeed have its roots in the tragedies your family has experienced, but as I have suggested it has become something else. This is now about you and your way forward into a positive future.

God's love casts out fear, and in him there is no death only more life after we pass over. Ask your guardian angel who presided over your birth to take away your fear. Perfect love and light casts out fear and once you lose this fear life at its fullest potential is yours.

Subject: **Spiritual Money Spinning?**

Aura Soma Bottle #33 (Dolphin- Royal Blue/Turquoise) enhances clairvoyant ability and supports all things psychic.

Dear Sarah
I am fascinated how you can tell so much about someone from a letter. How is it possible to help people you have never even met? Also I have put a lot of effort into my business pioneering an 'alternative' product. Will it pay off?

Believe it or not it is possible to send healing energy to someone even though we are not in their company. We all do this every time we pray. Of course nothing beats prayer, but there are also visualisation techniques that may increase your effectiveness. This does not mean that creative power allows us to manipulate things to our liking. Divine Will usually has a more measured agenda, which may pass us by if we are too fixated on manifesting our heart's desire.

There are serious lessons to be learned for those who attempt to step beyond the loving confines of God's will. Frequently people are attracted to the spiritual path by the concept of abundance, believing that adhering to certain disciplines will bring riches. This invariably gets blocked. Many of us are still living out deeply ingrained vows of poverty that equate money and material goods with evil. So cut those ties, and believe that you are entitled to abundance on all levels by the grace of God.

Sometimes we try too hard to make a success of things, when what the universe requires is simple trust. Your angels are available to you at all times, so ask them for help. But do not forget your own responsibility to yourself. God helps those who help themselves. Always remain grounded and reserve your judgement, particularly with finances. It is a mistake that a lot of people make. Just because a business is loosely based around the alternative trappings of spirituality, its success is not guaranteed.

The spirit world may have a completely different plan for you. These lessons are about remaining open and surrendering our little will (ego) to the greater will (God). Trying to trick the angels into what we believe to be our divine right does not wash. They work for our better good at all times so don't be conned by false promises. You will make greater strides if you hand your project over. Give up trying so hard and ask your guides if this is really what you are meant to be doing. Remember things are never quite as they seem.

Subject: **Developing Power**

Aura Soma Bottle # 7 (Gethsemene- Yellow/Green) brings no limits to a person apart from those set by themselves. Bottle # 78 (Crown Rescue- Violet/Deep Magenta) allows the full power from above to come to earth to assist humanity.

Dear Sarah
I am very interested in developing my spirituality. How can I be more powerful? Is it possible to be more psychic so that I can make good decisions? Are there any training courses you could recommend?

What a loaded letter! I am a bit worried about the way you link spirituality and power. True power is not the ability to manipulate situations at will. Any attempt to manipulate the universal order will inevitably backfire. It is not a good idea to attempt to bend things to your liking.

A fundamental law of the universe is that anything we send out by good or bad intent returns to us threefold. It might seem to be attractive to have magical power, but true magic happens when we connect with our higher self and respect the divine will.

When people are at the height of their spirituality they have surrendered ego to the universal flow. This is not an easy concept for most of us. What happens to little old me? The beauty of this surrender is that we do not get swallowed up in some cosmic tidal wave. Rather we become more fully ourselves.

Living without an agenda is a truly liberating experience, but it takes a lifetime to perfect. The truth is we never manage it fully. The intent is what counts. Really any action inspired by love is an expression of our spirituality. Buddhist monks spend lifetimes perfecting obedience by sweeping paths. This may be a strange way to reach nirvana, but the achievement is the open heart.

Great care is needed with the psychic world. It is not something to be tampered with. Again it should not be about ego. Degrees of psychic ability may be described as artistry. We can all paint a picture if pushed. It is the talent that makes a great painting. So we all have a measure of intuition that may certainly be developed. But it is dangerous to aim for power if you have the skill of visions.

The Gift is designed to help people, but like anything it can be used for good or ill. Remember the road to hell is paved with good intentions. Sometimes it is better to keep the simplicity of trust. The divine plan is devised for us to connect with pure Christ consciousness. What more do we need?

Incidentally a great by-product of true spirituality is heightened intuition. It is possible to receive messages through meditation and prayer. Really there is no need to go and buy a deck of tarot cards in order to sort out your life. "Them upstairs," as I call them have it all in hand. Sometimes it is a mixed blessing to know the future. Indeed it can be more a burden than a gift. People see something they want a piece of and this can be draining. In many ways you are better off keeping your own counsel and enjoying your life in peace.

Subject: **Karmic Career**

Aura Soma Bottle # 40 ('I Am'- Red/Gold) will allow you to establish your boundaries and tolerate no nonsense.

Dear Sarah
I am troubled by events that are making no sense. There is a situation at work involving some powerful people. I am confused by what is going on. On the face of it everyone seems charming and plausible. But I am experiencing feelings that have no logical explanation. Is there anything I can do to sort this out?

I appreciate that I cannot be specific about the details of your situation in this public letter. But the field in which you work is one of enormous importance. It is crucial that your colleagues are pure and true and maintain their integrity at all times. If this is not happening the entire company should be challenged and questioned. It is very important that you remain true to yourself in this situation. If you find you are compromising your own power it is time to quit. Your work is making you physically sick. You need to cut ties with certain individuals. They are unconsciously draining your life force. The reasons for this are karmic.

I know it is very difficult to get your head around the concept of previous lives. But believe it or not I do not think the existence of karma contradicts Christianity. In essence karma means that one receives what one gives. It is not unlike the biblical concept of reaping what you sow. Karma may be healed and absolved. Even the legacy of negative previous lives may be transformed by Christ's power.

This situation is challenging you to take a stand against the times you were destroyed by people who thought they knew best. When we incarnate we have agreed the terms and lessons of the life ahead.

This means that at a very unconscious level we all know what is going to happen to us. Significant events ring true for this reason. The challenge in being human is that we agree to develop and grow within the restrictions we have set ourselves.

Being both conscious and creative with our lives enables us to reach the heights.

Christ's power elevates us to our fullest potential. That is why in spiritual work it is so important to be true. Anything built on less than the truth will flounder and die. There is no place for ego in your line of work. So it begs the question - Why are these challenges of power and control in your face the whole time?

If your work continues to feel like an energetic struggle you should review your life. Right livelihood should energise and invigorate your system. Because it is not built on truth your place of work will actually close before the end of the year. But perhaps you should not hang around that long anyway.

Damage limitation should be the order of the day, so get healing and use protection. Otherwise you are in danger of being swallowed up in an elitist cult-like mentality.

Subject: **Past Lives**

Aura Soma Bottle # 47 (Old Soul- Royal Blue/Lemon) helps deep wisdom from the deep past to connect with the present time.

Dear Sarah
Doesn't a belief in Past Lives contradict Christianity? I am active in my local church with a simple faith. I do not understand how you can be a Christian and live many lives. Don't the laws of Karma contradict Christian faith?

I do understand your confusion because in many ways I still carry the same questions myself. I was brought up in a Christian home where we lived the spirit and joy of the gospel. We were taught that we are loved by God and known to him by name. A simple faith and trust was all we needed to cope with everything life might throw at us.

I still believe this to be true, but there are many complicated issues that arise along the way to challenge complacency. It is one thing to attempt to be wise as a serpent yet innocent as a dove, quite another to achieve it.

Working with psychic information is like walking through a minefield spiritually. I would be the first to admit it is akin to wobbling on a precarious tightrope. But the grounding of faith may help to keep us stable.

New Age spirituality claims to expand our consciousness by a revival of ancient belief systems. But does it inevitably contradict Christ's message of grace and liberation? It can do but it does not have to! I believe that the awareness of our road to enlightenment is developing. The exciting thing is that although everything we have been brought up to believe is true, there is more. Christ's redemptive action is still pivotal to our salvation. But our consciousness of what this means is becoming more sophisticated.

The New Age talks about Christ consciousness, the higher self and the master within. The importance of keeping spiritually safe is still very much an issue. On analysis these are a more fancy way of restating the Christian message. Christ dwells within and we become the best we can be in human form. So according to both the church and certain manifestations of the New Age we achieve our fullest potential in Christ.

As for past lives, for a long time I had a great problem with this concept. It does not sit easy with me and yet I now believe past lives are a reality. I guess we can be fearfully and wonderfully made every lifetime! This is where grace and karma meet. The knowledge and love of Christ gives us the chance to break free from the bondage of karma. Karma may be healed and it may be transformed.

Christ's death on the cross was the biggest universal karmic absolution ever; and yet we may still incarnate through many lifetimes to process our issues and expand our consciousness. The indwelling Christ brings our enlightenment, and I believe we will come to realise that all belief systems are in essence the same. It is the distortions of the truth that cause the rifts and the aggravation.

We are living a very exciting time.

CHAPTER ELEVEN:
Relationships

Subject: **Waiting To Hear**

Aura Soma Bottle # 3 (Atlantean Bottle- Green/Blue) nurtures the communication of the heart and brings peace.

Dear Sarah
I had a great chat with a guy on the phone who is an acquaintance of one of my friends. He is very busy but seemed interested. Will he get back to me?

This guy will get back to you in his own good time. Men are not always very quick off the mark when something is not their idea. He is interested in you and enjoyed the chat, but he is not particularly open to a relationship at the moment. His work commitments are top of the list and he has some major obligations to fulfil. However no job is worth passing up the chance of love for and this chap will wake up one day realising that success is not enough.

Subject: **Romance**

Aura Soma Bottle # 28 (Maid Marion- Green/Red) assists someone in breaking free from being a victim or a doormat.

Dear Sarah
Would you please read the cards for me about romance – every bloke I go with seems to use me and hurt me. Please Sarah, could you tell me is true romance on the way?

Firstly, I think it is very important for you to lose the expectation that you will get hurt. A lot of our most negative thoughts can turn into self-fulfilling prophecy if we allow them to. I think you should try to put the past experiences behind you. Don't dwell on them as bad times. Remember the positive characteristics of each guy, and try to convince yourself that they have some redeeming qualities! Relax and enjoy life, and learn from the relationships you have had. Every connection has a life span. It is the quality of the time spent together that is important. It is not necessarily good to hold onto something that has run its course.

At the age of forty-eight you might feel you have had all your chances. This is not the case. If you can adopt an attitude of fun and playfulness once again, you'll surprise yourself. The most important thing is to avoid an air of desperation. Men are attracted to independent, self-sufficient, and interesting women that leave them with something to think about. Display some vulnerability and flutter the eyelashes.

There is actually a friend or acquaintance that admires you. He may not be an obvious choice but he is a kind and gentle man. You have been in his company several times recently and the attraction has already begun. Does he frequent the local pub? Be open to different types of friendship, and you will be surprised what comes your way. It is better for you to build trust through companionship, than to rush headlong into a romance. You will find happiness, and be very content and settled by the age of fifty-two. There will be a significant relationship developing this year, so take your time and make friends. This way you will avoid giving away your power to the heat of the moment. Good luck!

Subject: **Commitment Issue**

Aura Soma Bottles # 3 (Atlantean- Green/Blue). Bottle # 88 (Jade Emperor- Blue/Green) help support emotional issues. They help you identify your true feelings and act accordingly.

Dear Sarah
I have been in love with a man for three years. He was happy to sleep with me and not commit. He eventually split with his girlfriend but when I declared my feelings he asked me to stay away as he didn't want to hurt me! Can I exorcise this guy? Should I move abroad?

Unfortunately, you have fallen for a guy who is clearly not available to you emotionally. He slept with you because he fancied you, and men find it hard to turn down someone who professes to love them. It tickles their ego! You clearly believe this man is a soul mate, and no one else can measure up. However, contrary to popular belief it is unusual to find happiness with someone who consumes our energies to such an extent . There is often a lot of karma in play.

This guy has been controlling your feelings and misleading you. He is not comfortable with commitment. Of course he feels guilty because he knows he has already hurt you. He simply does not want to be reminded of the fact! It is not usually a good idea to give an emotional display to the Peter Pans of this world. They simply cannot cope with raw feelings for all their macho sensibilities.

On a positive note there is a wonderfully passionate relationship for you by the age of twenty-eight. You will marry very happily, and your first child will be a boy who is very athletic and ambitious. It is a good idea for you to travel abroad again, and I think Sydney, Australia would suit you. Your reading shows clearly that in order to leave your disappointments behind you need to physically separate yourself from Ireland; at least for the time being. Your new man is very fiery and charismatic. He is a hard worker, and conscientious. He is of mid-colouring with large eyes, a straight nose and a rather surprised look. At first you will be cautious of him as he seems rather too smooth, and overly friendly. However he is genuine and charming. He will be showing you a good time before you know it. You will be able to forget Mr Wonderful, and he will come to regret that he missed out on a good thing.

Subject: **Prison Release**

Aura Soma Bottle # 70 (Vision of Splendour- Yellow/Clear) helps shift a feeling of being trapped with nowhere to go. Bottle # 10 (Go hug a Tree- Green/Green) helps the user connect with nature and to find personal space, however claustrophobic their situation.

Dear Sarah
Will I get out of prison on my review date in July? Are my girlfriend's kids mine? Will I be able to turn my life around and stay off drugs and out of trouble?

Without going into the gory details, I can see that you have been through a lot. On your release from prison you have a responsibility to yourself to turn things around. Firstly you should work on your fitness. If you can become obsessive about keeping fit all the better. You have understandably struggled with resentment and depression, and the regime of a physical discipline will suit you. It is a good sublimation for your anger. You have the determination and tenacity to make things right. I feel that there is an understanding counsellor or social worker available to you. Ask for their support. Announce the changes you want to make as this will work well for you when the review date comes up. Do not be afraid to make the most of the opportunities on the inside. Follow any chance to study, train, and offer help. You need to give evidence of good behaviour.

I think you would do well to cut the ties with the people you know, and the area you were living in. It would be all too easy to fall back into bad habits a few months after your release.

You need to give yourself a fresh start. I do see all sorts of incentives for you to get on track. By the time you are thirty-two, you will have great peace of mind. You will marry happily, and have a girl and a boy. Incidentally I do feel there is a boy around already. You could always ask your girlfriend to clear the situation up. Write to her about your plans for the future, and see if she will move to a different area with you The south side of Dublin by the sea would suit you; possibly as far out as Bray. Keep your cool in the situation, and do not subject her to the third degree.

I will do some long-distance healing for your situation. Believe it or not, there is a technique for sending energy that is as effective as being physically present.

Be patient and stay hopeful. There is no need to torture yourself any longer. There are no mistakes only lessons. The authorities will be assessing your situation soon enough. So smile a lot, and grovel.

Subject: **Love For Bouncer**

Aura Soma Bottle # 28 (Maid Marion- Green/Red) help to prevent you being walked all over by a man! Bottle # 11 (A Chain of Flowers- Clear/Pink) will inspire peace of mind and unconditional self-acceptance.

Dear Sarah
I am 15, and in love with a bouncer who is 27 and has two kids with his girlfriend. He recently kissed my best friend. He asks me if he should leave his family – but I keep saying no. Help!

But you do not keep saying "no" do you? You mention other flings with bouncers, and why are you working in a bar? I do not want to be boring, but this is both underaged drinking and illegal sex. I know that you are a mature fifteen, but you have many years of life ahead of you. It is unfortunate that you have had to take responsibility for your siblings. You have done well and been very kind to them.

Your mum will have to sort out her own problems. Emotional distress is the main reason that she drinks. I feel that she is very sad and stressed. You can help her on a practical level, but she has to pull herself out of this. Professional help will put her on the road to recovery. You must now take responsibility for yourself.

This guy you love is sweet in his own way, but he is easily led. Can you trust him? Can his girlfriend trust him? Can your best friend trust him? Can you trust her? I think you get my point. You deserve better than this ball of confusion.

If he wants to leave his partner so be it. She is not the easiest of characters, but she does have reason to be upset. Hormones in young mums do not make for rational behaviour; so she will kick and scream until she is heard. You must urge this bouncer to get his act together. He must decide between you. I think that your conscience gets the better of you, which is why you don't want him full time. You also know that your whole life is yet to come. There might just be something less taxing around the corner. No not a taxi – another man!

Incidentally, I think you would benefit from further training. A college course or government assistance scheme in hairdressing or beauty. You are more creative than you think, and it would be good to go for something that grabs your interest; but not any more bouncers.

Subject: **Loneliness**

Aura Soma Bottle # 47 (Old Soul- Royal Blue/Lemon) will help shift bitterness and energetically assists some -one to make the best use of opportunities. Bottle # 21 (New Beginning for Love- Green/Pink) will allow love to pull you through.

Dear Sarah
I am 49 years of age. My heart was broken in 1979, and I am afraid I will always be alone. I don't sleep well, and suffer from asthma. I am puzzled why I am lonely when there is so much love in my heart. Will I find romance?

You say in your letter that you used to be religious, but now you are not so sure. What did you expect from life? You are clearly aware of the limitations of your environment, and with your friends now departed, you are more isolated than ever. Life does not owe us anything, and sometimes it is up to us to make the changes that will bring in new opportunities.

Have you thought of moving to London to be near your best friend? I know you are a country lass at heart, but why do not you think about what life in a city might entail. I gather that the man you were in love with still lives locally. If you have feelings for him why don't you tell him, or at least develop a friendship with him? This will enable you to leave the past behind one way or another. I think you need to challenge yourself to take bold decisions.

There are many love relationships out there, and not all of them involve romance. Sometimes life does not provide us with marriage, kids, and family commitments. What freedom you have. Why not try and be more upbeat about your situation? You could do anything: go on a cruise, visit Lourdes, stay in London for a few weeks.

There are blessings in such personal freedom. It does not have to be a burden. Learn to enjoy your own company, rather than put on a brave face to the people you meet. If you begin to radiate self-respect, relationships of all kinds will present themselves to you.

Do not be afraid to be alone. We are all equally part of the Universe, and part of each other. Life will surprise you if you let go of your negative expectations. Do not limit yourself. If you trust and pray, the right path will unfold. God has not forgotten you, but sometimes we can get so wrapped up in our own fears that he cannot reach us. Enjoy the rest of your life, and do not feel guilty about doing something unusual or apparently off the wall.

I sense a great sense of companionship for you into the future, if you do not make judgements too readily. There is a coach tour in particular that will bring a romantic friendship into your life.

Try and organise trips and outings with a religious connection. The people will be open and accepting, and you will feel like you have an extended family. Community life would suit you, but I do not think that means taking your vows. It is time to relax.

Subject: **Insecurity In Relationship**

Aura Soma Bottle # 75 (Go with the Flow- Magenta/Turquoise) helps us accept things as they are. Bottle # 20 (Star Child- Blue/Pink) will help you let go of fear and love unconditionally.

Dear Sarah
I was told by a fortune teller two years ago that my boyfriend would do the dirt on me with someone from his past. I love him very much but I am insecure and can't sleep at night – I imagine him with my friends and other people I don't even know. Please help me I can't get past this.

I was horrified to read your letter. Some things are better left unsaid. Your boyfriend is not likely to sleep with an Ex, but you are fast on track to making it happen.

Some prophecy can be self-fulfilling. It is the responsibility of a reader to discern whether or not their insights are helpful. I am not saying that psychics should cover up the truth, but I am angry on your behalf. This prediction was not a good idea considering your temperament and disposition.

Autosuggestion is a powerful weapon and some readings implant thoughts in our heads that should not be there. I do not believe that your partner is inclined to be unfaithful. But I do believe that you could create the doubts in his mind that would cause him to be so. Do not expect him to stray, keep him on his toes, and concentrate on the positive aspects of your relationship.

Remember that you do not own him, so if there are aspects of his life that he chooses to keep to himself you must respect that. There is no point in trying to keep someone by second guessing their every move. This is a question of trust. If you find that you cannot trust him, despite the fact that he has given you no reason to doubt his love, you should move on.

It is important to take the man we love at face value, however well we think we know his weaknesses. There is something to be said for learning the way that men think. Be his friend as well as his lover. When he goes out with his mates ask if he had a good time. You could even ask what the talent was like! He is much less likely to look elsewhere if you keep him guessing yourself. Hold onto a bit of mystery and let him wonder what you are up to. This is a great way to keep a relationship fresh.

Sometimes when we are needy we project negative expectations onto our loved ones. They are not deliberately going to hurt us but our belief that they will encourages them to do so. I am not suggesting that you become a total pushover, but do relax and accept that you are loved. Betrayal is not inevitable so do not blow this chance of happiness.

Subject: **Confused Emotions**

Aura Soma Bottle # 88 (Jade Emperor- Green/Blue) helps us clarify our true feelings and emotions.

Dear Sarah
I am really confused. My Ex has asked me to marry him. Since we split up we have had an open agreement – an on/off thing. The problem is I think I have fallen for a married man in the meantime. Help!

Mm! The path of true love rarely runs smoothly. In a way I think that you and your 'Ex' were kidding your selves. You did not really split up! I'm never convinced that open relationships work very effectively. We are essentially monogamous beings who need to know we have divine rights to our loved ones. Slight exaggeration, but exclusivity is very important.

It is possible to have unusual agreements where each partner is allowed to have discreet encounters. But show me a person behaving like this who is happy? The boundaries are impossible to define in open relationships, and it is only a matter of time until one party falls for someone else.

You both had the right idea in one respect. By remaining available to each other you were leaving the door ajar. In theory there was always a 'bolt hole' you could run to whenever new connections got awkward! This noble arrangement did not give any one a chance. In one way you were able to provide each other with support during the break-up. But in another, you were sabotaging new love before it got a chance to take root. They do say better the devil you know. But in reality, you were both afraid to lose the one person you knew you could rely on (even in confusion).

The irony is, you are now closer and even better friends than you were before. So, what to do next? It is interesting that in the middle of this chaos, you fell for someone completely unavailable to you. I do believe you have very strong passionate feelings for this man, and a past life connection. Unfortunately, this does not inevitably mean you will be together.

Your decisions at this point are crucial. You have seen that nothing can break the daily bond you have with your Ex. You are great friends and there is an easy flow of companionship between you. In days gone by that would have been all you needed for a contented marriage. But times have changed, and we now expect a lot from a relationship. Our standards are high, and we often fall into the trap of believing *one* person will bring us everything we are looking for.

It is rare if not impossible to find a long-term love that has not faced these issues. Certain psychologists believe that polygamy is a more natural state of affairs. Fortunately, our society respects the status of coupledom. For some lucky people this brings fulfilment for eternity. For others, it is a most unfortunate arrangement that compounds their restlessness and signs them up to a life of torture. There are many still running around trying to find what they are looking for.

Follow your heart and mind until they agree with each other. Any decision is good if you follow it through. Things could get tricky and messy if you drag this out. So be brave, and do the right thing.

Subject: **Failing Marriage**

Aura Soma Bottle #81 (Unconditional Love- Pink/Pink) helps self-esteem and inspires Unconditional love for oneself and others.

Dear Sarah
My new marriage is already falling apart. We clash all the time…he is Taurus and I am Aries. He spends more time with his family and friends than me. Sometimes he doesn't even bother to come home. Will a child save our marriage?

Firstly *do* stop panicking! I understand how stressed you feel, and don't want to belittle your suffering, but all is not lost. Your husband is being very cold and detached at the moment. This must hurt deeply and be very distressing for you, especially so early in a marriage. At the time when everything should feel blissful and full promise, you are left wondering if you even have a future together. Life can be very cruel and you are being challenged in a profound way. Exercise as much trust as possible in your Guardian Angel and you will be surprised how things turn around.

The woman in me wants to say good riddance to your husband, and I know you feel the same. He has hurt you in a very unreasonable way, especially with his personal comments. There is no excuse for his insensitive behaviour; and this has been both cruel and undermining to your self-esteem. However there is hope for you both. You will have to muster all your powers of forgiveness and concentrate on the good aspects of the relationship. Look closely there *will* be some- you did marry the man.

Build on the positive aspects of the relationship and do not buy into any negativity. You can leave that bit to him. Without sounding too dramatic something has got a grip of your husband and is making its best attempt to divide you. I feel your man is quite depressed, and needs time to heal. Give him some leeway and step back. Too many more negative attacks and you will have had enough. So do not allow the rot to set in completely. It is better not to communicate, than to verbalise bad feeling. If you take on much more resentment the marriage will be destroyed beyond repair.

Your husband has deep seated issues to process and at present needs to be left to his own devices. Give him the time and the space to work through his nonsense and assess things for himself. You have pledged your life to each other for better or worse. It is highly unfortunate that your 'worse' has come along so soon.

Use reverse psychology in this situation. If you adopt a cooler, could not care less attitude, your husband will rally around fairly quickly. In a sense it is playing a game to pretend that you don't care any longer. But if you want to win this man's attention, the best way is not to contact him. Ironic I know, but the more you look for a reaction. The *less* likely you are to get one.

Play the waiting game and do not be so available to him. He is behaving very selfishly and does not seem to know his own mind. Therefore the more you push for him to honour his commitments, the more you will push him away. No man likes to be told how to behave or what his priorities should be. So back off or ship out altogether. Please do not even think about a child yet. Wait a while and let things settle between you first. Nature has a way of 'rumbling' things, and it is quite unlikely you would conceive with all this in the air. Children *do* bring healing and a new perspective. But things are a bit too precarious at present. It would be quite unfair on all of you to plan a pregnancy at this stage- do not even *think* about trying to keep him by having a baby.

Subject: **Lack Of Trust For Partner**

Aura Soma Bottle # 9 (Crystal Cave- Turquoise/Green) will help you search the secrets of your heart and find the answers.

Dear Sarah
I have a beautiful new baby. I should be happy, but I cannot explain the distress I feel. My husband has to travel abroad next month for work and I am sure he is going to meet someone else – he is always surrounded by beautiful women! I need your help please....

I can see that your fears come from a variety of sources. First your partner's lifestyle is not conducive to giving a woman the best feeling of security. You have to remember that in the music business a lot of things happen on a superficial level that shouldn't be taken too seriously. Egos learn to crave attention, and often act in ways that would mortify their mothers. However, I feel that your partner has been genuinely moved by the birth of his daughter. This event will prove that his loyalties lie with you. I do not think that he wants to go for one minute, and I think if he could, he would break his contracts to be with you and the baby.

You do have the tendency to worry yourself about things that will never happen, and having just given birth you are more vulnerable to this than usual. Be assured that your man loves you and wants to be with his child. You need to keep a level head. Do not expect the worst as that puts out unhelpful energies.

We can turn our lives around by thinking and acting positively. Keep your cool, and enjoy the personal space you have. Use the time to recuperate and look after the baby. You have a lot of support and good friends.

Your man needs to work to maintain his interests into the future. If you support him you will reap the rewards in more ways than one.

Subject: **Sister's Husband**

Aura Soma Bottle # 26 (Humpty Dumpty- Orange/Orange) will ease the emotional shock. Bottle # 45 (Breath of Love- Turquoise/Magenta) will assist give and take in a love situation with deep healing for the heart.

Dear Sarah
I am writing to you because I am worried about my sister. About a month before Christmas she heard rumours about her husband and another woman. He has since left her. She is heartbroken. They only adopted a baby 8 weeks before he walked out. Have you any advice to give her or can you see any light at the end of the tunnel?

You are right to realize that life does not always run smoothly. We are all here to process our issues, and to manage the best we can amidst adversity. None of us has a clear path from start to finish, and what does not break us definitely does make us stronger. Cliches aside, your sister really has gone through a difficult part of her life. But things should turn around if she can disconnect from this man.

Thankfully the child is not of his bloodline so she has a great chance to leave him behind. It does not take much imagination to appreciate that he was not the right man for her. I actually think that he got swept along by events at the time of the wedding without being sure within himself. He needs to step back and reassess his own path. I do not think that he was keen to adopt a child, and unfortunately the stress caused by the miscarriages only heightened their difficulties. This understandable grief meant that the marriage broke down. I do not think he intended for things to get so miserable. Through no fault of their own things fell apart.

It would take a great effort and commitment to salvage the situation. Your sister has a lot to forgive. I do not think he is a bad guy, it's just that things got out of hand. I feel that he now thinks he got married prematurely. He likes a lot of attention and the preoccupation with having a family did not suit him at this point.

There is a positive fresh start for your sister and your family is wonderfully supportive. I think her body rejected the pregnancies because she knew there was something fundamentally wrong with the marriage.

There is no physical impediment to her having children. She will really enjoy this new baby, and I believe she will be pregnant again very soon. Her true soul mate is yet to come, and she will feel quite liberated in time. She has been through the most difficult part of her life. If she can relax and trust that no man is better than the wrong one she will be fine! As soon as she is content with her independence and shows the ex she is stronger than he thought her life will flourish.

Subject: **Stifling Marriage**

Aura Soma Bottle # 46 (Wanderer- Green/Magenta) will help a person find their personal space plus appreciate the small things in life!

Dear Sarah
I am trapped in a marriage that stifles me. On the surface everything is fine. The children are happy and my wife is a good mum. Inside though I am falling apart. I have strong feelings for another woman. Does she still love me?

Ah the other woman! The answer is that she does still love you and she is in as much distress as you are. She has respected your status and even though she knows how you feel, she is as stuck as you are. There is no easy answer to a situation like this. Gracious people honour their commitments, but there comes a time when living a lie gets messy. Do you have the courage to break free? Which is more important your heart or how you are perceived by the outside world?

When you follow your heart with conviction everything falls into place. There is no point in doing the right thing if that is what is destroying you. Your wife knows you like the back of her hand. She is determined to keep you. That is her prerogative. She is aware you love women but she knows how to warn them off. In many ways she provides the stability that you crave but at what cost to your soul?

You need to think this through and then act on your decision. It is not fair to keep the other woman hanging on. She has put her life on hold in many ways because she believes in your love. Can you handle it? There is no resolution to this unless you are true to yourself. You need to work out what that means. You will not lose out if you make the right choice. You do not have anything to prove, and your biggest challenge to date is to make a bid for freedom. You will find that your popularity increases because you are happy. You do not have to feel a failure. The end of a relationship is always sad, but sometimes it is healthier for everyone to feel the winds of change.

It is important to remember that if you are courageous this situation has an end. If you drift on and continue to bury your head in the sand, the outcome may not be pleasant. This is your optimum time to decide who you are and whom you want. Be clear and go for it. Your family will be fine if you stay or if you go, but you may not. For once put yourself first. You do not have to carry the world on your shoulders. In fact you will be more effective when you are no longer fragmented emotionally. For everyone's sake be brave.

CHAPTER TWELVE:
Parenting And Family

Subject: **Wayward Son**

Aura Soma Bottle # 57 (Pallas Athena- Pale Pink/Pale Blue) helps us to let go and trust. Bottle # 22 (Rebirth Bottle- Yellow/Pink) helps us gain a new perspective and to live in the here and now.

Dear Sarah
I am worried about my son. He walked out on his wife of 16 years and left 3 children behind. His wife is now seeing her nephew in law, and my son has met another woman from a broken marriage. He is inside at the moment as he unexpectedly got into some trouble. Will we all be happy again?

Your son was actually unhappy in his marriage for longer than the final year. He remained for the children and tried to maintain the status quo for an easy life. He had problems related to work and money that he needed to sort out.

Unfortunately, as you mention he got into trouble with the law. The family situation caused him a lot of stress and grief. He did leave suddenly but it had been building up for a long time. He has found happiness with his new woman, and his wife resents that. For you and your husband it is a messy scenario but the next generation often face unexpected shifts and changes.

The pace of life has revved up a notch and marriages do not necessarily last a lifetime any more. I think that your best route to contentment is to accept the new situation and get on with your own life. No amount of well-meant interference is going to change things.

Actually your son's spell inside has been good for him in a way. He has had the space to think and get his head together. He really will be a reformed character when he is released. He is determined to be happy and sort out his life, and genuinely misses his new partner and his children.

His release date looks a little uncertain at the moment, but he will soon be made an offer that will lead to his freedom. At times he is a little down and a better fitness regime would help with this. He had a choice to pick himself up or go under. It is thanks to his new love that he fights on; so perhaps it would be good to be well disposed towards her. Taurus time will be significant for you all, and there will be major changes for the better.

Tolerance is the key, and turning a blind eye to the resentments of your daughter in law would be a good idea. Continue to look after the grandchildren and keep things sweet with their mother. She is content with her new man. She just thrives on a bit of drama. There is a trip abroad for you and your husband, so it might be timely to book those tickets. You need a break after all the upset. Things will naturally calm down for you, and this tricky situation will have a happy outcome. Life produces complex challenges, and sometimes it all seems to happen at once. Such chaos often produces dramatic healings, and miracles. I expect to see a great turnaround for you all soon.

Subject: **Holiday Romance**

Aura Soma Bottle # 21 (New Beginning for Love- Green/Pink) connects with love in foreign lands and will bring trust and a fresh start into matters of the heart.

Dear Sarah
I have a 22-year-old daughter, who wants to find a steady fellow to settle down with. She met a Spanish lad in May when we were on holiday. He told her every day that he was in love with her. We were only home 3 weeks when she moved over to him. A week after they split he went with another girl. She hopes to get back with him, but has to come home at the end of the season.

Oh dear, have you never heard of the holiday romance? The intensity and passion that resembles the real thing but evaporates before you can blink? A guy who tells you too quickly how he feels is rarely to be trusted. There is something to be said for the strong silent types who feel deeply and keep endearments to a minimum. At the point you wrote this letter to me you were obviously concerned for your daughter's future happiness. I can assure you she will find her own life partner in her own time and in her own way. You will be a grandmother to some delightful grandchildren.

Your daughter's fortunes do indeed seem to lie abroad, and I think it is a good idea for her to work abroad again whenever she can manage it. A deep part of you is holding onto her and monitoring her progress romantically and other wise. She was obviously shocked and hurt by this Spanish lad's behaviour and the experience was important. I hope she retains her innocence and trust in love, but it is also important to wake up a little. It is known that the hormones of young lads are riotous, never mind the added ingredients of sun, sea and sand. There is a heady concoction guaranteed to make babies.

I know she was also hurt by a couple of Irish lads, but what the Irish have in spades, the Mediterranean's have in buckets. I think it would be advisable not to move quite so quickly next time. There is a strong possibility she will hook up with this Spaniard again. But please remember how he transferred his affections within a week.

Your daughter might want to question the sincerity of his feelings. Just because a guy says he loves you doesn't mean it is true.

Words come easy, especially when sex is on the horizon. It is the actions that speak volumes, and I don't mean in the form of romantic gifts. You can keep the roses, chocolates and presents. What counts is the real thing. Love that is not afraid to remain centred in the midst of life's difficulties. Sure we all love a bit of romance, but love should not be bought with words and gifts.

The real deal is fearless, committed and steady with plenty of passion thrown in for good measure. Your daughter will find this. A relationship that gets better as the years go by, rather than one that evaporates when something tantalising crosses its path. Boys will always be boys, and while that is happening I suggest your daughter has some fun. She will marry a man not a boy, and the children will be the making of him.

Subject: **Worries Re Future**

Aura Soma Bottle # 23 (Love and Light- Rose Pink/Pink) inspires compassion, tenderness and self-acceptance however difficult the life path. Bottle # 81(Unconditional Love- Pink/Pink) it helps you to love things the way they are.

Dear Sarah
My life has always been a mess. I have brought up 8 children almost on my own —with a bad husband. I'm separated 12 years. Will I get my money worries sorted out? Will I meet someone who will care about me? I also have problems with a 17-year-old daughter who is pregnant by a 30-year-old man – he stays on the dole to avoid maintenance. He is not a nice person. Can you advise me?

I think it is a great shame to dismiss your life in one sentence like that. You have clearly put up with a lot of difficulty, and you should pat yourself on the back; eight children is a great achievement. You need to start to give yourself some time and attention. You must make sure that your ex pays his way with the upkeep of the family. Why do you have to pay all the bills? Get your rights sorted out in the courts if you have to.

You need to leave your daughter to make her own mistakes at this stage. You cannot be expected to carry everyone else for much longer. She will soon be a mother herself, and with that responsibility will be forced to work out her own priorities. She has chosen to get involved with this man, and you must respect that. It is her destiny to work this out. There is no point in passing judgement on either of them. Try and let the situation go. They live together at the moment, and they are both adults. It is best to leave them to it.

Be supportive of the grandchild by all means, but try not to interfere by persuading her to leave him. It is time for you to pamper yourself for a change. As much as possible try to develop new hobbies and interests. Join an interesting evening class. Can you get yourself abroad with a sister or friend? There is a high possibility of you meeting a new love in a different country. How about a coach trip to Scotland or a pilgrimage to Lourdes?

If you can let go of your worries as much as possible, and expand your horizons with new experiences, you will find peace of mind. You have to get yourself out there, to meet someone worthwhile, and I think a common interest is going to spark romance between you. All the best.

Subject: **Family Problem**

Aura Soma Bottle # 74 (Triumph- Pale Yellow/Pale Green) will help brings clarity into difficult emotional situations. Bottle # 44 (Guardian Angel- Lilac/Pale Blue) will transform negativity into peace.

Dear Sarah
I am disturbed by the behaviour of two of my brother's. They blank me and avoid all communication with the family. We don't understand why. Is there anything I can do about this?

It *is* heart-breaking when the people we love ignore us, but I think you have a good idea why this has happened with your brothers. You get on just fine with your other siblings, but you are carrying a burden of responsibility for these two. You are the family peacemaker, and you are the most sensitive about this issue. The others are not too pushed about why the brothers have evaporated. One is older than you and the other younger, so you are quite literally primed to be piggy-in-the-middle.

Deep down inside you know that it was your mother who alienated her boys. She could not handle the pressure of difficult adolescents, and your father would discipline them accordingly. Your older brother is prone to depression, and has felt misunderstood and stifled for much of his life. He prefers his own company, and is wary about trusting people. He does think about you in particular, but tends to be paranoid, so after all this time is not likely to make contact.

The younger brother is weaker, so he was often on the receiving end of misplaced anger that should have been directed at the eldest. Your parents did the best they could, but they were quite narrow-minded and intolerant. A lot of kids under the same roof of course necessitates some discipline, but life was always presented as a struggle against the odds. Where was the fun and laughter?

Complicated children need to break out of such a restricting atmosphere and find their own way. This is the risk all parents take – what freedom should they allow, and what is an appropriate amount of discipline?

Your younger brother will reconnect with you when he finds a permanent relationship, and security. It is not up to you to force the issue, but you should tell both brothers how you feel. If you are patient and honest with your feelings the universe will bring the response you need. You must leave them to it once you have said your piece. Such situations require you to let go of the past and move on.

If you are meant to have a fuller relationship with these brothers they will find you at the right time. Unfortunately you are a reminder of the past they have tried to leave behind. Men tend to be brutal if they cannot handle a situation. It is easier for them to behave as if it does not exist. They hurt themselves in the long run, and it is when they realise what they have done that the healing can take place.

You cannot force a complicated situation to a point where it can be healed; it really is a question of patience and time.

Subject: **Parenting Issue**

Aura Soma Bottle # 80 (Artemis- Red/Pink) will help you let go at the appropriate time to allow loved ones to find their own way.

Dear Sarah
I am concerned about my children for different reasons. Will they sort themselves out?

There comes a time when parents have to be a bit philosophical about their children. Giving them up to the universe is not easy after years of hard work and caring, but it is what is required. They have to make their mistakes, and find their own way forward.

Having said that your youngest daughter is unsettled, and obviously still needs your guidance. She has grown up before her time, and is a little wired by the energies of her brothers. Her real education will be the travel she does at the age of sixteen to seventeen. She does not have much fun at school, and in many ways does not see the point of study. This is unlikely advice, but you would benefit by giving her more credit.

Try and steer her curiosity about the big wide world, towards an interest in other countries. She would connect very well with Spain, and the Spanish way of life. Do not be afraid of her travelling to live and work abroad. It really would be her salvation.

Your eldest daughter has gone through quite a lot of insecurity in her marriage. All will be well if she can be less demanding and more of a friend to her husband. There is a good change of work for him in time that will ease his own stresses and strains. Children will save the day: a lovely girl, and boy. If she can be a little more independent and trusting, her husband will curb his behaviour and realise how lucky he is.

You mention that your sons have a gambling and drinking problem. Are you sure it is as bad as you think? I would not have any concerns about the eldest as I feel he will be very successful with money. He will marry very happily which gives him the opportunity to leave depression and difficulty behind. I am most concerned about your youngest son. He needs your love and support. For some reason he feels a failure, and he needs his self-esteem boosted.

Try not to put conditions on your love and do not make harsh judgements. Be on hand with a big hug and good food. It sounds rather quaint but I feel he wants his mum to go easy on him. He will sort himself out but not quite in the ways you expect.

Your worries as a mum are not unfounded, but do try and give yourself some quality time. Let go and trust that all will be well for your family. Sometimes we can attract misfortune by concentrating on the negative aspects of our lives. So, book yourself a holiday, and realise that your loved ones will make their own way for better or for worse. Very little happens that is not predestined – if anything.

Subject: **Parenting**

Aura Soma Bottle # 80 (Artemis- Red/Pink) helps with letting go.
Bottle # 82 (Calypso- Green/Orange) helps someone find a new direction in life.

Dear Sarah
I am devastated about my daughter. She does not want to know us anymore. She was a lovely girl growing up, very thoughtful and good to us. About ten years ago she met this fella and he seemed nice enough. Unfortunately she moved into his home, we were very upset and kept after her to come home, so she then had nothing to do with us. What do you think we should do?

What a shame you did not take advice about this all those years ago. I know that as a parent it is very difficult not to have expectations of your offspring, but there does come a point when you have to surrender these. Unconditional love does not really go hand in hand with being human, but there is something to be said for letting go.

You mention that you have prayed about this until you are blue in the face. Perhaps you should give up your anger towards God as well. Prayer is not some form of magic that we only use when we want our own way. Neither is your daughter deserving of your love only when she is towing the line. She clearly needed to break free from the constraints she felt to make her own mark on the world.

Sometimes we can smother the things we love to the point where they have to run or die. I think your daughter was bored and depressed. Of course this is not your fault, but she needed to do something to create her own boundaries. She did not have any control over her life, and as a feisty character she needs to run her own show.

I think that the only thing you can do now is to go quiet on her and keep your dignity. This present situation is not the end of the story, but you have to accept that you may not get your daughter back. As soon as you do this, you will get your daughter back! This is a test of your faith, and the psychology of not giving a damn any more will reap dividends. She keeps running because you keep pursuing. You are indignant, and this energy does not help.

Unfortunately you feel that she owes you something, and equally unfortunately, she feels that she does not. Both of you are wrong, and there is stubbornness on all sides. Really any future relationship has to be on a completely different footing. I believe that the arrival of grandchildren will help. She will get more of a sense of how difficult it is to be a parent, and you will by then be much more cool and detached.

If you can, forget that she is your daughter and think of her as an adult and an equal. She has made choices that you might not approve of but which you must respect. I hope this does not sound harsh, but I have a feeling that if you ignore her next rites of passage: birthday, Easter, and Christmas, the situation will turnaround. An odd suggestion, I know. But sometimes reverse psychology is the only way.

CHAPTER THIRTEEN:
Soul Mates

Subject: **Where Is My Soul Mate?**

Aura Soma Bottle # 24 (New Message- Violet/Turquoise) reels in your soul mate. Bottle # 46 (The Wanderer- Green/Magenta) offers a new beginning for love.

Dear Sarah
When will my Soul Mate materialise? I know who he is but I am fed up waiting! I yearn for the companionship of a relationship. I'm not too bothered about the romantic bit, but wish I had domestic bliss with someone.

One of the pearls of wisdom that my father passed onto me was that there are many potential relationships out there. In fact he often said that he did not envy the abundance of choice open to the younger generations.

Because of the numerous options available to us, it is perhaps a bit limiting to expect perfection in the form of a soul mate. We tend to idealise the notion, and demand that the outcome be happy. We carry the belief that there is only one person who can possibly bring fulfilment, and are devastated beyond repair if it all goes wrong. Of course we need our dreams and fantasies up to a point. But it is when they start to invade reality that they become hazardous.

Unfortunately a connection with your soul mate does not guarantee happiness ever after. These scenarios are usually less than straightforward and in fact they can be quite heart-breaking. It is common to have quite negative situations with a soul mate. Usually they are not available. There are frequently frustrating issues that have to be addressed and resolved.

It is not unusual to become entangled in a fixation that gives endless fodder to our anguish. The person concerned may be quite oblivious of our feelings whilst we merrily feed a fantasy with every gesture he makes in our direction.

Unrequited love is in fact a lot more frequent than we would care to admit. I have noticed we like to jazz it up with the 'Soul mate' label!

The people I see who are finding it hard to let go of someone are usually on a path towards self- discovery, if only they would wake up and smell the coffee. It is in fact unconditional love that we crave: the freedom to love ourselves and others without all kinds of restrictions and expectations. Never was a truer word said: if you love someone, let them go. Surrender the person to the big wide world. If they are stupid enough to stay away, that is their loss. You need to keep a bit of dignity.

Why strive to win the heart of someone who is clearly not interested? For two soul mates to come together there has to be an ease of communication, and equality of consciousness. The other person may not remember that you were blissfully happy together centuries ago. If you are meant to be with this person in this life, love will win through.

But remember you cannot force someone to wake up if they wish to remain asleep. They may have commitments and loyalties that are tying them up.

Sometimes out of love you must respect their decisions, which may not be the most romantic in the world.
For a love to make sense beyond the boundaries of your own mind, it must be grounded in the practical world. Having said that if your soul mate loves you but does not have the courage to act he will remain sad and lost. If you truly are soul mates then you will find completion in each other. No one else will do. It is getting past the obstacles of our modern lives that will make or break this situation.

Subject: **Teenage Angst**

Aura Soma: The energetic vibration of Bottle # 24 (New Message- Violet/Turquoise) attracts your soul mate.

Dear Sarah
I'd like to know Sarah – what does the future hold for me? Will I be happy in the future? What will my career hold for me and am I destined to find that special girl (my soul–mate) soon?

You say in your letter that you have had an eventful love life, and you are not yet seventeen. You should relax about finding your life partner and enjoy your youth. I do see plenty of passion and heartache in your reading – you are in line for quite a varied string of relationships. Having said that, you will know your soul mate when you meet her. She is tall, elegant, dark, and slim. She will resemble you in many ways, and could pass for your sister. You will marry happily, and have children – but you should take things easy and enjoy your friends, male and female. The right girl will not pass you by. She just might take a little while to appear. Follow your instincts in your relationships and you will have fun in the meantime.

To succeed in your chosen career of sports commentator you will have to be determined and tenacious. It is always advisable to follow your dreams, and you will win through if you persist. A three-year course at college is good for you, and I recommend that you study computers and commerce subjects as a safety net. A career in television could take a while to materialise, and I think you would be successful on radio first. Make sure you research sports as a hobby, and build up a good knowledge of history and facts of your chosen sport. Follow the techniques of other commentators, and listen to their coverage regularly. This way a lot of their training will reach you at an instinctual level.

You will be happy if you can learn to be content with the present moment – live each minute to the max and enjoy yourself. Do not stress yourself out with missed opportunities. What is for you will not go by you. One of the most annoying phrases ever, but true nonetheless.

Subject: **Desperation For Love**

Aura Soma Bottle # 81 (Unconditional Love- Pink/Pink) inspires a person to love themselves and others unconditionally.

Dear Sarah
How will I…when will I…where will I…will I ever…Fall in Love???

Firstly, lose the obsessive phraseology! With that amount of intensity and desperation you will chase your opportunities away. Do calm down, take a deep breath and relax. I want to ask you what is the big rush? You are young with your whole life ahead of you. I know you have a lot to give and a lot to receive but do reassess your priorities for the moment. For some people it is more important to focus on career, family, and self-development first.

There is a school of thought that believes you do not really connect with your Soul Mate until your own personal balance and equilibrium has been reached. There is no age restriction on this. You could be born a fully integrated personality (unlikely), or you may not even get close to what Carl Jung called "Individuation" in this lifetime.

Do not panic. This does not mean love will elude you, but it does mean that you may find relationships and yourself a bit of a challenge. Life is the sum total of our experiences, so our difficulties are just as significant as our triumphs. Remember that what threatens to defeat us may also set us up. The choice of how we respond is the test of our character.

There are many kinds of love. Every relationship is different and leads to a unique connection and feeling. It is therefore quite difficult to define exactly what love is. I know you are anticipating the stomach churning, heart palpitating head-rush sensation.

Addictive it certainly is, and some people spend their lives pursuing this fix. But ask any pensioner, these pleasant sensations have a shelf life and they only mark the beginning of what being in love really means. I don't mean to be a killjoy, but maintaining a healthy relationship takes a bit of effort, compromise and commitment. Shirkers need not apply.

You are clearly looking for the first love experience…and I assure you that it will come, but only when you stop looking. Do remember that teenage/puppy love is often more about yourself than the object of your desire. It provides a delicious learning curve, which puts you in touch with what you are really looking for. And which if you are blessed goes onto to develop and stand the test of time.

Unfortunately, in our modern culture there is so much diversity and temptation. If you manage to maintain your first romance I will be duly impressed. It can be done, but often these connections fall prey to parental caution, career pressures, and endless opportunities.

If you are lucky enough to find true love at a young age, hold on for as long as it makes sense to *you*. The likelihood is that you will change, develop and possibly grow apart. But always follow through your feelings. People reach maturity a lot quicker these days, so make adult decisions and stand by them.

Following your heart, whatever your age can never be wrong. Do not let the fear of failure spoil your opportunity for happiness when it comes. You are highly intuitive, so trust that and forget the analysis. Your youth does not exclude you from the chance of happiness. Quite the opposite as you will experience heightened emotions and intensity of feeling. You are nowhere near "comfortably numb," and the rotten stench of cynicism has not yet left you jaded. I say go for it when love arrives. You will know all about it all soon enough.

Subject: **Love For A Pop Star**

Aura Soma Bottle # 10 (Go Hug A Tree- Green/Green) helps you cope with the feeling of loneliness, and 'too much personal space'. It supports all heart issues and helps you to connect with nature.

Dear Sarah
I think I'm in love with a guy in a pop band. He drops hints on how he feels but is always working. Will we be together? I want to marry him and have his babies.

You obviously have a crush on this guy, but it is not really a match made in heaven is it? You know how unavailable he is and his commitments are work, image and making money. He does not have the space for a relationship and spends his time fishing. Of course he is a lad what would you expect? He is of an age where anything is possible and needs to leave all his options open. This kind of situation is very difficult for young girls who have all the romantic notions of love, marriage and babies with the first guy they meet. It is all part of growing up.

Of course dreams do come true; do not get me wrong. This fella is attracted to you and really likes you. He also thinks about you quite a lot, which acts as an escape valve from all the work he has to do. The link between you both is strong, but I do not think you should have high expectations at the moment.

This guy is thinking long term, and he knows he has plenty of time to find a mate. He wants to explore all his options and is quite happy to have a few encounters along the way. You may indeed be one of these if you want to be. But try to be realistic and realise that you are both young with your whole life ahead of you.

There are so many possibilities open to younger generations now. Settling down is not so much of a priority, particularly to the lads. Us girls have to learn to adjust to the situation, and play them at their own game. He will find you more attractive if you are less available to him and he has to chase you for a reaction. The thrill of the chase! Be a mystery to him and this will keep him interested.

This guy is very clever and knows how to leave a girl dangling until he sees her again. He will give you just enough of a hint that he is interested, which keeps you interested. Do not be taken in by him completely as there are a few love interests in the air for this looker.

One point in his favour is that he does not play the field. This guy is keeping his options open, and you are one of them. He does not take advantage physically, as he is not able to. In a way you have reason to be confident if you can keep his interest, but you also have to be patient.

Be aware that this lad can be a bit slippery if he knows you like him, so don't come on too strong or he will run. He needs to feel he is running the show and has the say so in what happens. Feisty, dominant females need not apply.

There is certainly something about you that grabs his interest, but he is in a dilemma. In a way the situation confuses him, as he didn't want to fall for someone at this point in his life. Part of this guy doesn't want to get real – he needs an escape route. But sure, you can't help who you fall in love with, can you. Now that is quite a romantic thought. Love will win the day.

Subject: **Mixed Messages**

Aura Soma Bottle # 87 (Wisdom of Love- Coral/Coral) helps to process unrequited love and complex emotional situations.

Dear Sarah
I am really confused about this guy I fancy. He gives mixed messages – sometimes he seems really keen and at other times he ignores me. Should I wait around or walk away? I am in a long-term relationship, but can't stop thinking about this other fella.

I do not think guys realise the affect they have on us females half the time. When we really like someone, we think about them, dream about them and merrily scheme the next scenario. Things never happen quickly enough, and we never seem to get the answers we need soon enough. You are caught up in this spin, and need to relax. Most guys are very straightforward, simple creatures who like to keep things as uncomplicated as possible. Anything for an easy life. I am sorry to any males who take offence and to those who thrive on intrigue, dishonesty and infidelity.

I would be naïve to state that what you see is what you get, with all men. But life will be easier for you if you adopt this belief, at least until the incriminating evidence appears. It is probably true of most, and to the rest we will give the benefit of the doubt.

There is no point in trying to second-guess this attractive Romeo. He will make his intentions clear, and if he does not move on. I know when you are holding passionate feelings for someone it is the most difficult thing in the world to ignore them. But sometimes for the sake of other people and your own dignity, it is the best thing to do.

I may sound like Auntie Sarah at this point, but no guy is worth your attention if he messes with your head. To blow hot and cold is a tendency people have when they are uneasy, unsure, or feel under pressure. However, he is not deliberately trying to wind you up and he is actually quite shy. Remember you are expecting quite a lot, especially as you already have a boyfriend.

Much as he likes you, Romeo cannot take it further. Admittedly he has been rude - there is no need to ignore someone, however mixed up you feel. But do understand that until you make up your mind, not much more can happen.

To connect with this guy you feel passionate about will mean relinquishing your current relationship. I do not believe you really want to do that; correct me if I am wrong?

Thinking of this attractive guy has given you something delicious to fantasise about. Do be aware that the reality would play out quite differently. Can you live with things as they are? In one way it is not fair on your boyfriend to walk around with such intense feelings for someone else.

There are many types of love and passion is certainly the most compelling. However, be careful not to mistake intense physical attraction for love that will last. Of course the connection could develop into lasting bliss, but it may not. Do you really want to throw over your childhood sweetheart? You may indeed have outgrown each other, which is why you have drawn this new person towards you. But do be sure that you do not fall between two stools emotionally.

Remember, if someone really wants you they will move heaven and earth to be with you. Obstacles melt away and everyone else can like it or lump it! Call me an old romantic, but nothing will stop real love.

CHAPTER FOURTEEN:
Unrequited Love

Subject: **In Love With Counsellor**

Aura Soma Bottle # 87 (Love Rescue- Coral/Coral) helps release you from the torture of unrequited love.

Dear Sarah
I am married since 1945 and have three adopted children. My husband and I have been going through a very hard time these last 10 years. I am a really anxious person. I have strong feelings for my counsellor, and was devastated when he got married. A fortune-teller told me that she had never seen a reading like mine. Everything that could have gone wrong has done so.

Will you please stop blaming yourself for what is wrong in everybody else's life? Your three adopted children will find their own way forward, particularly as they are now adults. It is part of every young lad's experience to get up to mischief and to experiment with substances they shouldn't go near. Obviously the degree of being naughty will vary, but a youngster needs to privately work out his own boundaries. You can only offer your parental guidelines and appropriate discipline, then hope for the best. You are right. Obsessively breathing down the necks of your children helps no one. This is not another excuse to beat yourself up. What is done is done. It is now the time to move on with your own life, and surrender your loved ones to the divine parent in the sky.

It is really important for you to get to the bottom of your own heartache and sadness. Your counsellor will help you achieve this. It is very common to have strong feelings for someone who is helping you in this way. It is this man's job to ensure that his professional behaviour remains scrupulous.

You are right, the fact that he got married is really nothing to do with you. He has compassion and feels empathy for your situation. It is not healthy for you to harbour feelings for him. I would actually recommend that you change your counsellor at this point, so do put in a request to that effect with the hospital.

It is actually possible to become too reliant upon those whose job it is to help us. Tough love at this point would cut you lose. You may no longer need to pour out your heart. My feeling is that you need healing and times of quiet and relaxation. Sometimes words are not enough, and a few sessions pampering yourself will work wonders.

I will keep you strongly in mind when I do my long distance healing sessions. You will become more independent and relaxed. It is important to find your own power at this point in your life. It will be a process that will naturally unfold for you.

Start to have a bit of fun. When you are angry and frustrated express those feelings then move on. It is okay to cry. When you are depressed it is common to cry on a daily basis. The way through this is to accept this is the space you are in.

Do not fight against the things that cannot be changed. In the times we are living in it is so important to savour and appreciate the good things in our lives. We may not have all the things we ever wishes for, but we do all have a measure of hope to play with. I can assure you that the more you relish the positive things in your life, the more they will multiply. We attract to us the events and experiences we expect. So lighten your load and expect the best. That way you will bring some magic into your life.

Subject: **Pregnancy Problem**

Aura Soma Bottle # 28 (Maid Marion- Green/Red) will give you the strength to leave and stop being a victim.

Dear Sarah
I was going out with a guy and he left because I could not get pregnant. I am now with someone else, but because I cannot get pregnant he is arranging to do a contract marriage with a white lady. I have to understand the situation. She does not know about me, and if I complain he gets rough. Is it worth staying in this affair?

By first reaction to your dilemma is run. Get the hell away from that man! However I know it is not as simple as that. When you are stuck in a situation it is not always easy to see a clear way out. I do think that you should work towards leaving this man as soon as you are able.

It is not good to stay in a relationship that is so undermining to your self- esteem and happiness. This man is not only using you he is making you believe that he is doing you a favour by staying with you! You have started to believe that you cannot do without him, and he intimidates you so that you cannot question his behaviour. He has also conned you into believing he is helping another woman get her papers. If this were the case there would be no reason why she would not know about you. He would benefit financially, and so would you. There is more to that relationship. She believes he loves her.

Although I do not condone marriages of convenience they are fairly easy to organise particularly in London. He does not need to visit her repeatedly to make the arrangements. He is having a long distance relationship with this woman. He is using her as well as you. My guess is that he wants money from this situation. He is totally selfish and out for himself. I do not believe that he loves either of you.

What makes you so sure that you cannot have a child? Never say never I have met many people who were told that they could not conceive and still did so. Also there are opportunities to adopt and foster children, but of course the environment has to be right.

You are getting things the wrong way round. A healthy relationship is about the love and respect of two people, not about a woman's ability to multiply. You are not a baby machine. Leave this man. He is not right for you. He is controlling and undermines your personal power.

I see a happy marriage for you in the future and a different perspective on relationships. Lose the belief that you do not deserve to be happy. You are a charming woman with a lovely smile and a wicked sense of humour. Attract a decent man with colourful clothes and your naturally mischievous personality.

Not all men want children and it certainly should not be an issue that preoccupies your mind so much. Relax. There is a man out there who will love *you*!

Subject: **Powerful Attraction**

Aura Soma Bottle # 84 (Candle in the Wind- Pink/Red) helps both you open up to love and say goodbye to the past.

Dear Sarah
I am strongly attracted to someone who is not my long-term partner. Ironically he is showing interest in me again after years of complacency. I think I have fallen for this other person but do not know if anything will come of it. Do I pick up the pieces or move on?

They do say that once a relationship has been eroded by complacency and emotional neglect there is no turning back. I agree in principle but it is very daunting starting afresh when you are used to having someone around. Never mind how outworn that pair of slippers at least you know the shape and feel of them. A big part of you has accepted the status quo of the comfort zone and you are terrified of making a mistake. Fair enough, but why not live dangerously in this instance? I think you will regret it if you ignore your heart and hormones. Nature has a way of giving us strong clues when we are stuck in this way, so do not be afraid to follow your instincts. It does not matter at all that he is younger; after years of famine a feast is yours for the taking.

Make an intelligent decision about your partner and honour your integrity. You are not passionate about him because he has hurt you deeply, so it is not surprising that you cannot respond to his advances. Perhaps it is time to take your cue and move forward with your life. There are no guarantees in love relationships. If you play the game and take the risks you acknowledge the life force within you.

If you want to settle with Mr Slippers and step out of the game be aware that inertia and numbness may set in. Sooner or later the decision will be the same, except you will have passed up the chance of excitement and happiness with this new fella.

You are definitely at an important cross roads in your life, so take your time. There are no mistakes in life, only experiences that become the sum of who we are. The more you have lived the more interesting and desirable you are so please do not judge yourself as a failure. Be confident about the road ahead as you know the correct guidance lies within you. Remember your partner never suggested marriage or family and in many ways he enjoyed the ride minus commitment.

Do not get hooked up on these issues, as the guy who is right for you will offer you his hand without any hassle. You will not feel stifled or cornered, and unusually neither will he. Your soul mate connection brings with it an ease that you do not have to question. If a man is doing your head in, you can be fairly confident he is playing out a karmic link that you should disconnect from. When a man challenges and undermines you so that you feel uncomfortable and less than human: move on.

Subject: **Endless Waiting**

Aura Soma Bottle # 87 (The Wisdom of Love- Coral/Coral) helps ease the pain of unrequited emotions.

Dear Sarah
I have spent many years waiting for my former lover to leave his empty marriage. We are friends at least but I am troubled. The lack of physical contact is difficult to cope with. Will we ever be together?

It is amazing that you have both been able to remain friends in this situation. I suspect that in many ways you are bending over backwards to accommodate him. Clearly you do not want to blow the slightest possibility that he may eventually be with you. Fear of losing this man is holding you back in many ways. He is intelligent and kind, and of course found it impossible to cope with the stress of going between two women. I know you sometimes question his truthfulness. Is the marriage in fact as dead as he describes?

There are many types of connection of course. Yours is both cerebral and emotional. He loves your company and is still very attached to you. Unfortunately for you he cannot justify a physical affair. Although you must feel spurned and rejected, at least consider that his honourable behaviour gives you a better chance in the long run. As a true friend he has guided and helped you. So be thankful for the intimacy you still have. Any ultimatums or impatience on your part would actually damage the friendship. You need to either accept the status quo, or move on with your life.

Any experience of unrequited love is of course intensely painful. Count your blessings. Although the passion has faded between you, the relationship is still strong. The bonus is that it now has some integrity. At least you are no longer running around arranging passionate liaisons.

Do be aware however that emotional infidelity is just as much a threat to a marriage as a full-blown affair. In some ways this man now has the best of both worlds. Your companionship and loyalty give him the elements that are missing from the marriage. And most importantly to him he is no longer wracked with guilt. He can hold his head high and say there is nothing happening.

He overstepped his moral code by having an affair with you. That alone is testimony to his genuine feeling for you. So please don't ever think that he used you. However, you have got stuck where he left you...firmly in the past.

Understandably you fail to see that things have changed. Although you were indeed two consenting adults, this man has left you dangling in the hope of an eternity together.

Soul mate connections are rarely straightforward. There are a lot of issues to be hammered out before peace descends. Your challenge is now to adapt to the situation and be stronger within yourself. Independence of spirit is an attractive quality. If he senses that change within you, I do believe you have more chance of a lasting link. If you have to walk away to find your feet, maybe do so. But please explain to him your purpose to him as it will make him think.

Of course you are afraid that if you step back you risk growing apart. However, if you can no longer stomach his denial of what happened or his refusal to talk about it, you may have no choice. I would like to see his reaction if you disappear, as then he would have to face himself. As it is he has everything he needs. Think about it and make a good choice.

Subject: **Trapped By A Baby?**

Aura Soma Bottle #87 (The Wisdom of Love- Coral/Coral) helps you process unrequited love.

Dear Sarah
I do not know what to do. I am beside myself! I love a married man and I think he is interested in me. His wife recently had a baby so I think it's hopeless for me and him. He blows hot and cold so I don't know truly how he feels. Will we be together or should I move on?

Oh dear, it looks as if you have fallen for the charms of a man who is confused. He is a lovely man with a lovely energy, and would not have deliberately led you on. However, he is uncertain of his own future, and you have unfortunately got caught up in the saga. This man is very loyal and committed to his friends, so even if he does have strong feelings for you, you will feel left out. It might be wise to sit down and think about what priority he gives you.

At the moment you are nowhere on his list of engagements. You have spent long years being patient, and understanding of his situation and you are not someone who would normally hanker after someone unattainable. There is a strong bond between you and an understanding, even when you do not see him for weeks at a time. However, because you have been so kind, this man has not felt the need to make up his mind. He is a character who chooses to go with the flow of life, and to honour his commitments. So in many ways, much as he loves you, it would take a miracle to bring you together.

There is a slight possibility that his domestic situation will get on top of him. Underneath her aloof demeanour she is actually panicking. Because they have known each other for so long she has a strong sense he has fallen for you. There will never be pistols at dawn with this scenario, but there is one thing she could not forgive. Be very careful you do not get pregnant by this man. If you do she will throw him out. He will be all yours. Are you sure you want that? Do not forget he has stayed away from you despite himself. How encouraging is that for your future together? Be sure of your own feelings and you will be okay. When you are true to your heart, you cannot fail. Eventually the truth wins out. So if you are sure, your focus and patience will be rewarded.

Subject: **A Convenient Return**

Aura Soma Bottle #87 (Wisdom of Love- Coral/Coral) helps us cope with feelings of unrequited love. Bottle #25 (Florence Nightingale- Purple/Magenta) frees us up from disappointing experiences.

Dear Sarah
I hope you can put me on the right track in my life. I am separated from my husband. We get on ok. In the last two years I met up with the love of my life again after not seeing him for twelve years. We agreed that he would move to Ireland. He has children but is separated. Once he moved here, he cut me off completely. I need to know why.

I'm afraid that I do not trust this man. You need to think back to the reasons that you split up twelve years ago. Remind yourself of the feelings that you were left to handle alone. You grew apart, and the intensity of the emotion between you did not last. Once things cooled off, he made his exit pretty damned quick, and he did not consider you properly when he said goodbye. I think this man is very clever at saying the right things. He knows how to get his own way, and he knows how to work your emotions.

Geminis are very good at flitting from one thing to another. They are the butterflies of the zodiac. If you review your own behaviour with your husband you will see the echoes. You are wondering if you have been used physically, emotionally, and financially. Did you ever stop to think how your husband might feel about how he has been treated? By your own admission your husband was not the right man for you, and yet he has remained in the background as some kind of security blanket. Perhaps there is more between you than you care to admit? Why did you suggest that your other man would be better off in Ireland with you than near his family? Underneath it all, you do not trust him either. You were not willing to take the risk of starting afresh in London, because you knew this man would let you down.

Did it not strike you as odd that he voluntarily re-contacted you? In the meantime he separated from his wife. Did the coincidence not strike you? He seeks you out precisely at the time he is leaving his wife. This is not a man who likes his own company. To me he appears selfish. He is someone who will cover his tracks, plan ahead, and will not be left out in the cold.

Even Geminis who are in love can be notoriously unreliable in a social context. You would want to put them under lock and key to ensure they would never flirt again! They need to be loved with the full awareness that they attract the opposite sex, like moths to a flame.

There is no point in expecting the kind of commitment you are talking about from this man. He will need you again, having said that, so make sure there is some straight talking. May I suggest that you sort out your relationship with your husband, and free each other up? There is no harm in remaining friends, but why not allow each other to get on with your respective lives? It is important to sort this out legally. There is great peace of mind for you if you can be honest with both men. A sale of a property will bring peace of mind, and there is a renewed marriage contract on the horizon. A trip abroad would help give you the perspective you need, so that you can make these important decisions. Be direct and clear about what you want, and you can expect all this confusion to subside. The universe tends to reflect back to us what we put out. So clean up and you can expect clarity.

Subject: **Emotional Affair**

Aura Soma Bottle # 87 (Wisdom of Love- Coral/Coral) helps you process unrequited love. Bottle # 81 (Unconditional Love- Pink/Pink) inspires unconditional love.

Dear Sarah
I am devastated! The married man I thought I loved has completely wiped me off the face of his universe. How do I put this behind me and win out?

I would be the first person to agree with you that it can really hurt to be excluded from the heart and life of the man you love. But sometimes there is no other way, especially if there are too many significant others involved! When such a link has not been sexual it is difficult for some people to understand what the problem is. There was no affair. This is the web your man has trapped you in.
Do remember that emotional affairs can be just as devastating and the capacity for denial of the event is 100% for the man. Which is an unfortunate fact that leaves you looking back at years of wasted energy and false hope. You have certainly been led on and left dangling, but how would you ever prove it?

This man has been very nifty and self-serving. He has leeched off you emotionally, knowing you were there for him being quietly supportive in the background. It might be difficult for you to accept, but some of this behaviour was unconscious on his part; conveniently so I might add.

There is a subterranean aspect to the connection, which appeals to this man's sense of danger and intrigue. You have been participating in a merry dance: a potent but discreet astral affair. At the moment this man is playing the dutiful husband and has tried to put his antics behind him. Good for him, but where does that leave you?

There are plenty of couples who stay together regardless of attractions for other people. When there are children involved of course this makes sense. The likelihood of your man getting cold feet if things get intense is high.

A lot of married men are masters of denial, and if you challenge him on his behaviour, I guarantee you he will wonder what you are talking about. Why make a fuss, unless you have had enough and want him to run for the hills. Because this is a social link there is not much you can do. This man is arguably just flirting and expressing fondness for someone he meets now and again.

For the sake of your own survival it is probably good to try to objectify it in this way. I know it is intrinsically a lie, but you have to keep your dignity and kicking up will not help anyone. Time to be as altruistic as possible.

It is actually quite clever psychology at this stage to push him away by doing something unappealing and out of character. That way you can distance yourself from the situation and alienate him in the process. This to my mind is a better course of action than surrendering to the victim role. You can buy into his ostrich behaviour and bewilder him in the process. This is much cleverer than 'dissing' his name or creating a scandal.

Do remember that what goes around comes around. This man will need you very soon for more than just reassurance. For a long time you were an intimate link for him to draw on without the complications of a deceitful affair. But how honest of him was that? The tables will turn and you will then hold the power in your hands. Be as lenient as you have the mind to be.

CHAPTER FIFTEEN:
Media Issues

Subject: **Popstars**

Aura Soma Bottle #50 (El Morya- Pale Blue/Pale Blue) is very supportive of media work. Bottle # 43 (Creativity- Turquoise/Turquoise) enhances creativity in the Spotlight.

Dear Sarah
How was it justified that a psychic was used on the show POPSTARS? Surely asking the kids to go and get their cards read was an extreme invasion of their privacy? Are you qualified to do this work, and what gives you the right to set yourself up as some kind of oracle for the Irish Nation?

I obviously need to take this opportunity to explain myself. The Popstars programme televised weekly on RTE rubbed certain people up the wrong way. Parents in particular were concerned that these kids have subjected themselves to a traumatic ordeal. It is of course absolutely heart-breaking to see the disappointment of the rejected. But do not forget that all those who took part in the show knew exactly what they were letting themselves in for; and what a prize at the end for winners: everything they have aspired to and dreamed of falls into their lap. Not bad.

With Popstars the producers created a programme that was both ground-breaking and controversial. They wanted to add a unique Irish flavour to the workshop in particular. The director Lynda McQuaid displayed a breadth of vision most unusual even in terms of reality television. Bringing a psychic into a project like this was bound to cause waves, never mind ripples. There is something about psychic work that cannot be quantified. The data-base does not handle such information. A psychologist is fine; he has a certificate or two, so we can cope with him. But a psychic?

From my point of view this project was a stimulating challenge. The bulk of the work I did with both the kids and the panel is of course off camera. Believe me, there was even more controversial material assigned to the cutting room floor. The contestants did not have to come and see me, but they all chose to do so except one. The healing and clairvoyant work we did is private, but after the session their moods brightened.

Some people have reacted strongly about the immoral aspect of psychic readings. I would be the first to agree with you. As with all things there can be an immoral aspect if the skill is used for the wrong reasons. Just as priests have been known to abuse their position, so psychics can have a negative influence upon someone's life. I have written many times about the need for caution with all things spiritual that may not be coming from the right space. I can assure you there is nothing abusive about the work I do. I help, heal and guide people to the best of my ability. Oh, and this psychic actually does have certificates so we are laughing.

Subject: **TV Work**

Aura Soma Bottle # 43 (Creativity- Turquoise/Turquoise) is very supportive of those who work in the media world. Bottle # 96 (Archangel Raphael- Royal Blue/Royal Blue) helps you connect with your higher self to inspire integrity and balanced decisions.

Dear Sarah
I am a working psychic and I'm wondering if I should try to go into TV. I have done radio before, but I am uneasy about the TV. What does it involve? Will I be famous?

Being successful is one thing. Being famous is another. I feel it is okay to become famous as a by-product of good work, but not to look on fame as the measure of your success. I strongly believe that it is unhealthy to strive to be famous. Why do you need that attention? It is much more important to do your work with integrity and act responsibly towards your clients. Leave it to your guides to decide whether or not they need you in the public eye.

Radio broadcasting is a good way to let the nation know you are there, especially if you are used to working on the phone. But television is something else entirely. If you decide to do television as a psychic you must go in wearing your suit of armour. Not only are you up against cynical presenters who are anxious to fight their own corner, you also have to feel comfortable with the cameras. Psychically you are taking on a lot. You might be the most competent reader in the quiet of your own home. But subject yourself to the scrutiny of people who do not even understand what you are doing, and you are up against it! I have actually been asked "how do you know that?" a few times by a baffled presenter. Being pushed for time I just say "because I'm psychic."

There is no point in trying to educate the ignorant, but this urgency to catch you out is what you are working with. The producers want entertaining television. They are not too pushed about your fine-tuning. There is no time to think, and unfortunately this means that members of the public get short shrift as well. The psychic messages I get on television are to the point. This is unfortunate when people have important issues. Before you have even made your point the next caller is on the line, or your co-presenter is jumping on what you have just said trying to undermine it. Still want to do live TV?

The cut-throat world of entertainment and media is not an easy environment for a psychic to work in. At best there is a mild derisory tolerance from the cynics, at worst you are hung out to dry. Having said that if you are meant to work publicly your guides will protect you. They have a sense of humour after all, and you will often find that those who strike you down meet their own Waterloo in a rather interesting way.

CHAPTER SIXTEEN:
Healing

Subject: **Tony Quinn Seminar: Guru Syndrome**

Aura Soma Bottle # 55 (The Christ- Clear/Red) gives us the energy to follow our ideals.

Dear Sarah,
I am about to re-mortgage my house to attend a Tony Quinn seminar. Will the money return to me as promised? I don't feel it is a waste of money, but I do worry about the debt.

Sometimes there are more important things in life than money. If this seminar is the right thing for you, the money to take part will manifest. Lessons of value often have a price, and a significant exchange of energy must occur in order to reap major benefits. This could prove to be the best money you ever spent. The people I have met who connect with Tony Quinn have nothing but praise for his vision and energy. I certainly do not think the gift of inner knowledge is a waste of money. It is not that Tony Quinn sits down and hands out the key to wealth of body, mind and spirit. But for those who get the point he guides them towards the full use of their own inner strength. One of the laws of the universe is that we are made in the image of God. We are all creators of our own destiny. It is possible to tap into this creativity for better or for worse.

We are more powerful than we appreciate, and this naivety can be dangerous. Often our negativity and restrictive ways of thinking prevent us from achieving our fullest potential. The mind is like a cinema projector. If there is an undermining reel whirring in our head, the projected picture will not be pretty. It is important to lose the disaster scenarios that sometimes monopolise our thoughts. You can be sure that what you expect to happen surely will. It is all about focus. Some of us may have a belief that we will win the lottery. But if we are honest deep in the darkest recesses of our minds we do not expect to. We are therefore defeated before we begin. This kind of success is not supposed to be about money, but there is no reason why an abundant spirit has to go without. The beauty of focused energy is that we can be or do anything we set our minds to.

Ever wondered why it is that those who make something of them-selves have such self-belief? Simple. Nothing will deter the person who has something to prove to themselves and the world at large. Apply this focus to spiritual issues and you have a very special energy indeed. It should not be about ego, but it should be about being the best we can be. Nor does it bring a license to trample over everyone who is in the way of where we want to go. Unconditional love for ourselves and other people will more than compensate for the fact that we remain human.

Unfortunately attending a Tony Quinn does not a Superman make. You will still be functioning within the bounds of a human mind and body. However, the insights that such training brings will turn your thinking around and therefore your life. Don't panic it is not a form of brain washing! There will be great respect shown for who *you* are. You do not have to accept something that does not make sense. So reserve judgement and come home a new man.

Subject: **Shock And Panic**

Aura Soma Bottle # 26 (Humpty Dumpty- Orange/Orange) is very effective with all kinds of shock. Bottle # 42 (Harvest- Yellow/Yellow) should support you with anxiety and worry.

Dear Sarah
About a year ago, three of my 'so-called' friends jumped on me from behind! It was such a shock and I don't think I've recovered. I'm currently in sixth year but dropped out due to this. I suffer from panic attacks and I am attending counselling. Will this work out? Will I conquer this?

You will be fine, but you are indeed still suffering from shock. I am horrified at your mates. They obviously thought it was funny to traumatise someone more sensitive and vulnerable. It's called bullying and I hope you reported it. I also hope they realise the trouble and anguish they have caused. It was an incredibly thoughtless thing to do.

Sometimes an event like this triggers a tendency that is already there within your psyche. My feeling is that you are questioning life and your place in it at a deep level. An identity crisis, alarming as it sounds, can in fact be a great gift that strengthens you for the future. Once you have processed these anxieties and fears you will be formidable.

Counselling can be a slow and laborious process, but it is worth persisting with the visits. You may not have a dramatic breakthrough, but the effects of verbalising your fears are enormous. If you can get hold of the Aura Soma product for shock, the Humpty Dumpty bottle, it would help heal the experience. Also the Bach Flower Rescue Remedy is brilliant for panic attacks. This is available from most chemists. Carry it around with you and take small drops until the feelings pass. There is also a pocket-sized etheric rescue bottle, No. 26 in the Aura Soma range.

Buy an amethyst stone and have it with you at all times for protection. This stone guards you against negativity, and is a crystal traditionally used to ward off danger. It also works closely with the crown chakra, which will help allay any fears lurking in the corners of your mind.

Please look into resuming your studies. It would be such a shame to let these idiots mess up your life more than they have already. College is a good idea for you, so perhaps look into finishing what you started elsewhere. You are bright, so use your intelligence and get back to the studies. You need to restore your social confidence as well as the irrational fears. This has taken a severe knock, and you will need good friends and support.

Do not be afraid to talk about what happened with friends. People who are truly for you will not have a problem listening. There is fun and happy times ahead, so put these so-called friends to one side. They do not really deserve anymore of your energy. I will do a cutting-of-ties for you that will assist you to move on and relax. Incidentally a yoga class would be excellent for re-balancing your energies. Please find a class, and develop confidence. I cannot over stress the benefits you will feel. Within two months you will be kissing your counsellor goodbye.

Subject: **Failed Pregnancy**

Aura Soma Bottle # 26 (Humpty Dumpty- Orange/Orange) is needed to ease the shock of the situation. Bottle # 11(A Chain of Flowers- Clear/Pink) to assist the conception of a child (the same soul that you lost last time).

Dear Sarah
I am in great distress. I suffered from a blighted ovum. This means my pregnancy did not develop properly. Why did this happen and is there another child for me?

It is not possible to provide a ready answer that explains the reasons why we suffer. But of one thing you can be sure - God has your best interests at heart. There is a divine plan in place that will make sense in the long run. This latest pregnancy was a shock to your system and in fact you were not ready to carry another child full term.

Mother Nature has a very special way of protecting new life and some people believe that souls waiting to incarnate change their mind if the conditions are not right. It is heart breaking to lose a child or even the idea of a child, and so you must take time to grieve what has happened.

It may be of comfort for you to hear that I believe your next child will be the same soul that aborted its last attempt. The brother of a friend of mine told her that he changed his mind four times on his way into this world. He had such a developed consciousness that he remembered his battle to be born. Their mother suffered four miscarriages between her birth and his which validates his story. I hope that this story cheers you up and shows you the promise of good things to come. I am confident that your next pregnancy will be completely straightforward. In fact by the time you read this you will be three months gone. We have talked privately, and you have done important healing work, so I am sure that it is full steam ahead for you with this one.

Be assured that your body needed to adjust after the birth of your first child. It was important that your system rested and realigned itself after some months on the pill. I would perceive the blighted ovum as a gift that in fact helped your body to right itself. You were given a dummy run, and heart-breaking as it was it has enabled you to carry a child full term.

Some times with sensitive systems the pill tampers with hormones beyond our requirements. After this baby there is no need to worry about the same thing happening again. What you experienced is a thankfully rare occurrence. Of course you will ask why did it happen. But if you look back and review the timing of that pregnancy and the now perfect timing of this latest child, you will understand why. Enjoy this baby, she is very special.

Subject: **Living With Pain**

Aura Soma Bottle # 26 (Humpty Dumpty- Orange/Orange) helps the system to assimilate all kinds of shock. Bottle # 54 (Serapis Bey- Clear/Clear) is very powerful at shifting negative energy and pain.
Bottle # 25 (Florence Nightingale- Purple/Magenta) helps to mobilise the body in convalescence.

Dear Sarah
Recently I attended a healer who I thought could cure my stressed nerves at the top of my back. I feel very upset and disillusioned. Will I ever shift the pain that I have lived with for years?

Firstly, it is very naïve to believe that there is always a cure. Some conditions are about management of symptoms, particularly if the stress is ingrained and you are used to living with it. As a healer myself, I can testify that miracles do happen, but they are not inevitable. Sometimes our healing process requires us to endure a situation that is ultimately to our benefit. There can be many complex reasons why suffering is prolonged. The reality is certain illnesses have the capacity to hold other people's attention and sympathy. Our identities can become quite connected with our latest aches and pains. This might sound harsh but some people are actually reluctant to be healed. The distinction between healing and curing is very important. A healer can for example assist a person to die in peace and with dignity.

Your own suffering relates to nerve damage around the base of the neck. I can see that you have great anger and resentment towards the medical profession. You believe mistakes have been made. The problem has quite literally become a pain in the neck! Massage is a treatment that would benefit you, and possibly acupuncture. In one sense you are fortunate that you can feel pain, as more serious nerve damage = paralysis. There is no deterioration in your condition, but it is important to find the remedies that bring relief.

You have a tendency to lash out in frustration and anger and you are holding fast to a belief that you are beyond help. Be gentle with yourself and others. The additional stress only knots you up. Ginko Biloba helps boost blood flow to vulnerable areas, and I suggest you take the Bach flower remedy Willow to relax your feelings of embitterment. Yoga would benefit you immeasurably: it can increase mobility, and help with misalignment in the spine.

The power of the mind to facilitate healing is legendary. There are many meditation techniques to bring pain relief and peace. Use the Reiki self-healing to help yourself. If we do not take responsibility for ourselves we over-burden others and lose the sympathy vote. You can do this . Your reading shows that you can turn your life around with determination and tenacity. I always recommend the absent healing skills of Saint John of God, based in Brazil. This can be booked on line visa the web site www.johnofgod.com.

Subject: **Drink Problem**

Aura Soma Bottle # 81 (Unconditional Love- Pink/Pink) assists the acceptance of difficulty with a compassionate heart. Bottle # 76 (Trust- Pink/Gold) helps us set the loved one free and to find our own potential.

Dear Sarah
I have struggled for years with anger and bitterness. 27 years ago I gave up two kids for adoption. My husband and I had two more that were taken into care because of my drinking. I am now sober, and receiving counselling. I feel so cheated by life. Can you help?

Your life has been so full of trauma and upset that counselling may not hit the spot. You also need healing. There are a lot of karmic issues in your situation, and the negative energies that have floored you need to be addressed. I will do some long distance healing for you over the next few weeks. Please continue with both your full-time work and the sessions. Both provide you with an important reality check.

 Thankfully you have started to move forward, and your physical difficulty with the drink is resolving. You must now start to disentangle the emotional stress. The anger, jealousy, and resentment that you experience started in childhood. Understandably you felt abandoned, and disconnected from your family. This legacy has caused repeated patterns throughout your life. You need to break the chain and move forward.

 You must forgive the people who have hurt you. Start to love and accept yourself. The crystal rose quartz, is very helpful, and there is an Aura Soma bottle (No # 81) called Unconditional Love. Remember that God never abandons us however low we feel. He is more than able to give us the support we need, whatever is going on in our human relationships. With him there is always a fresh start on offer – freedom from all the things that weigh us down.

Honour what your son has said in his note. He will indeed contact you when he is ready. Relax about the connection between your husband and daughter. Do not feel excluded, as they will open up to you if you stay cool. Always keep in mind that you are worth it – you are worth knowing, and loving. Give yourself some respect and so will others. It is not necessary to control either people or events (tempting but not wise!). All power to you.

Subject: **Agoraphobia**

Aura Soma Bottle # 31 (The Fountain- Green/Gold) helps you overcome deep fear. Bottle # 10 (Go Hug a Tree- Green/Green) allows you to find the space to do what needs to be done. The affirmation of Bottle # 7 (Gethsemane - Yellow/Green) is 'I have no limits apart from those I set myself'.

Dear Sarah
I am agoraphobic and have not been able to leave the house for 14 years. My friend helps me go out in the car occasionally, but I need to know will I ever be normal?

There is a lot of ignorance about agoraphobia. I believe that many cases are a manifestation of depression, rather than weird psychology. When you are depressed you are more vulnerable to external threats, and a fear of exposure is the end result.

Agoraphobics are hyper sensitive to any invasion of their space. This means that a stroll down Grafton street is impossible: all those eyes, all those movements, all those vibes! Put the same person outside a nightclub at 5am, and there will be no problem in walking home with ease. It is the overload of stimulation that produces the panic.

Understanding this is the first step on the road to recovery. Desensitising your self is the second. This can be a laborious process, but once you have begun there is no turning back. The fact that you are determined to succeed is the key to your improved health. Ask your doctor if he feels you would benefit from an anti-depressant, and then plan your strategy.

The most effective tactic is to make a list of everything that you consciously avoid. Put these in order of difficulty. Then proceed with the easiest task on the list. This might be a car journey up to the local shops with a friend. Get the friend to wait in the car while you queue for a paper. Do this twice a week until you can do it without thinking.

Another effective challenge would be a walk on the beach with the car in view. Usually it is comforting to start with places near to home. But see how quickly you can build up the distance you can walk. Every success will make you feel stronger and more confident. Sometimes you will feel disheartened, but even if you are only achieving a certain amount you must hold on to the fact that you are still progressing.

Believe it or not driving lessons are a brilliant idea, when you feel ready. Being in control of a car gives you the important sense of power that you lack. It is your own little world on wheels. You can go anywhere in time with a car wrapped around you! Also, perhaps your family would enjoy looking after a pet. Obviously only do this if you can make the commitment. If you decide to go ahead you will be amazed at the confidence walking a vulnerable puppy brings. Borrow a friend's baby for the same impact!

These are only ideas, but they are effective keys to unlocking your own strength. In time you will be amazed what you can cope with. Bach's rescue remedy is a brilliant prop to always carry with you. It helps just knowing it is in your pocket, and it is a great pick-me-up even if you are just tired. Another useful trick is hiding behind sunglasses. The shades block a lot of the stimulation that would normally bring on the panics. Try and manage without them, but when you are in a difficult situation, like in an airport, use them to full effect.

All the best with this, I went through it myself some years ago, and now I zoom around without a second thought. So treat the depression, and try the behavioural plan. You will be well in no time.

Subject: **Grief**

Aura Soma Bottle # 78 (Crown Rescue- Violet/Deep Magenta) helps the grieving process. Bottle # 11 (A Chain of Flowers- Clear/Pink) helps a woman conceive if the conditions are right.

Dear Sarah
Can you help us please? I was told by a fortune-teller that we would have five children. I am 37, and in October 1999 we lost a baby. We miss him so much. We have another boy, but will there be more children?

I can see from your reading that you have been through unimaginable grief and disappointment. After quite an idyllic start to your marriage and family life you have been dealt a tough blow. Difficult as it may seem to understand there is a gift in every situation. There is something about grief that connects us to the ebb and flow of life. Once the shock has been processed, and this can take a long time, we begin to connect with the oneness of the universe.

Somehow the healing of grief reduces the fear of death. If we were close to the deceased we have a sense that they live on. At times we are aware of their presence and they feel but a breath away. This whole experience forces us to face our own mortality and look directly at our own place in the world. It can ultimately be a liberating situation, but the road to freedom is painful. There are the pitfalls of anger, frustration, bitterness, depression, and we can get stuck at any point.

The key to tackling grief is to ride the roller coaster, and feel the emotions. There is no magic formula to make it disappear although certain healers and spiritual people can be of great help at this time. Unfortunately it is resistance which gets us *stuck in a moment*. We have to be brave and get on with our lives. Our loved ones are in a better place, of that we can be sure. So it is really our responsibility to them and to ourselves to fight on.

I feel that your baby is very peaceful. He is a sensitive and sunny character. He wants you to know that there is a baby girl on the way. After three years of grieving, this will give you the strength and the healing that you need. For some reason, I feel that the hill of Tara is of great significance. Please try to visit, as I believe that you will experience a wonderful sense of release there. Your equilibrium will return and you will want to embrace life once more.

By the age of forty you will feel that your family is complete in the best possible way. There will also be grandchildren to make you smile; at least five of them. I know that you have physical difficulties, but I believe with medical support and guidance you will conceive and carry a daughter. Your second son is very close to you, and I know that you are aware of this. Spiritual tranquillity is on the way, so follow your instincts and you will find it.

Subject: **Bereavement**

Aura Soma Bottle # 78 (Crown Rescue- Violet/Deep Magenta) for bereavement and psychic development.

Dear Sarah
I lost someone recently who meant an awful lot to me. I am worried about my reaction to this. I have watched videos of the deceased dry-eyed and smiling. I do believe I am a little bit psychic as well. I have had some accurate predictions in my own life come true.

Please do not be worried about the path your grief is taking. There are many reactions to death, not all of which are mournful. Some funerals are joyous occasions, particularly where the person has had an active faith. Really there is nothing upsetting about the assurance that our loved one is in a better place.

Negative grief reactions often reflect our own deep-seated fears and distress rather than worry for the departed. Of course we would not be human if we did not miss their company, but people who grieve are often given divine help. There are many stories of people hearing and seeing their deceased soul mates. At times of difficulty it is common to be blessed with a tangible sense of their presence.

I feel that you are receiving a wonderful confirmation that all is well with this person. Others around you are not so clear headed, but this does not mean that you are in some way detached. On the contrary, it is a great testament to the intensity of your relationship with this person. Sometimes we can be wracked with guilt rather than grief when a friend or family member passes on. You are free from this torture because your relationship was so fluid. You are not emotionally strange it is simply that there was no agenda between you. This is an opportunity to count your blessings and to live the rest of your life in peace. I feel that this friend will always be near you, guiding you and keeping you on track. Talk to them and ask for their help, and don't forget the power that comes from having God on your side.

As for your psychic experiences, I think we could all report one or two irrational feelings that have proved to be correct. We all have a measure of intuitive ability it just depends to what degree. It is nothing to be alarmed about. The rational mind does not have all the answers. There are many dimensions to our brain capacity. Just because something springs into our heads from nowhere, does not mean it is not to be trusted. However, do not make the mistake of believing every imaginative thought.

The real skill to being psychically aware lies in the interpretation of the message rather than the message itself. Some angels and guides have a wicked sense of humour, and frequently there is a twist that accompanies our major expectations. It is important not to invest too much faith in outcomes. It is the angels who carry the perspectives of eternity. At times we are guided to surrender our deepest wishes to divine supremacy.

Subject: **Fertility**

Aura Soma Bottle # 11 (A Chain of Flowers- Clear/Pink) boosts a woman's fertility and gives the best chance of conception.

Dear Sarah
My husband and I tried for over 5 years to have our first baby. In Dec 1999 we were successful with the help of the fertility drug Clomid. I fell pregnant again but unfortunately lost the child two months into the pregnancy. I would love to know if we will have more children.

I do feel that you fell pregnant quite quickly after your first baby. Perhaps you were on a roll! However sometimes nature will not be hurried along. I do see another pregnancy but after a gap of three Christmas times. Ask your doctor if there might be a new approach he could take. For some reason I am wondering about a different dose of the drug after a time of rest. Ask him!

On a practical level there are things you can do to help. Wearing rose quartz is said to help fertility. Why not buy a big piece for beside the bed? Also a wheat free diet will greatly help your weight. Substitute wheat with different grains, rice and potatoes.

Drink a lot of water to detoxify your system, and replace dairy with Soya products. Soya is brilliant for the hormones. A friend of mine was once told she would never have a child. Two years later after a rigid dairy and sugar free regime she conceived, without medical intervention. Dairy products are known to be mucus forming, and the effects of extra mucus in the system can block the fallopian tubes. Visit a medical herbalist to see if there are ways to tackle this problem differently. Make sure he/she is a legitimate practitioner.

Please check that any herbs that you take are compatible with Clomid. You might want to give your system a rest for a while. Ask your doctor if he would support the above diet and a break from the Clomid for a few months. I feel that it is important to relax and detoxify. I have a feeling that you might not even need the drug to conceive this time.

The child that you lost was a boy, except you did not lose him. He is around you very strongly as a guide, and in fact he is more use to you where he is. Sometimes souls that choose to incarnate change their minds. They start the journey into life, and decide they prefer it back home. If God wishes to bless you with another child I believe that it will be a boy. I think it is important to have this perspective sometimes for then we are not so attached to outcomes. There is a definite plan for your life, and all things happen for a reason. I feel that you will understand this very profoundly by the time your grandchildren come along. There is huge contentment in the future, so relax and trust that all will be well.

Subject: **Parenting And Personal**

Aura Soma Bottle # 3 (Heart Bottle- Blue/Green) is very effective with all complicated heart issues. It also helps with asthma.

Dear Sarah
I have an 8-year-old son to take care of as his father didn't want to know him. I have suffered with anxiety and panic attacks. Will I meet someone soon as I am 32 in July? Will I marry and have kids? Will my son do well at school as he has missed a lot with his asthma and tummy problems?

You certainly have a lot of uncertainty and worry to cope with. Start by counting all the blessings in your life. You ask if you will marry and have kids. You have achieved part of that already. Your son needs your love and attention and it is great that you have your parents to support you.

I think your son has a problem with food intolerance, so it might be worth getting him checked out by an alternative practitioner. Keep him away from foods which contain additives, and that includes some breads. If he has to eat sweets the kinder range of chocolates are good. Also avoid the fizzy drinks and drinks containing citric acid. You will have to turn into a label watcher to help your son. Dairy products lie very heavy on his stomach I feel, so try to get him used to Soya replacements that contain added calcium to see if there is an improvement. Avoidance of dairy produce will certainly ease your child's asthma and take up as many old carpets as possible, particularly where he sleeps.

In time your son may indeed want to know his father, which I think should be encouraged. You are understandably resentful of the way you have been treated. Believe me there is light at the end of the tunnel. Try not to worry so much about finances, as you will never want for anything. There will be more peace of mind when you marry and settle, as indeed you will. De-clutter your bedroom and keep your living area tidy.

To boost relationship opportunities introduce the colours red and pink and lose all shabby furniture. It is better to sleep on a mattress on the floor than an old uncomfortable bed. Write the qualities of the man you wish to attract and put them under a red candle by the bed. Light the candle every night to your future happiness and pray for peace of mind. Do not fall asleep with it alight!.

I will do healing for your anxiety, as panic attacks are a horrible thing to live with. The Bach Flower Rescue Remedy from most chemists is worth keeping in your handbag on standby. Take life a day at a time and lose the negative feeling that something dreadful is about to happen. Our minds are powerful and we can be our own worst enemies at times. Sort out the monsters in your head and the monsters in the big bad world will also go away. I may sound a bit naïve on this point, but you have every reason to be optimistic. Just relax about the future and trust your angels to guide you a heavenly route.

Subject: **Nasty Fall**

Aura Soma Bottle # 25 (Convalescence Bottle- Purple/Magenta) assists physical recovery. Bottle # 26 (Humpty Dumpty- Orange/Orange) will pick you up to start all over again!

Dear Sarah
Can you please pray for me? I had a nasty fall at home in the kitchen last year, no bones broken but they told me the pain could last a very long time. I pray a lot to God but he don't hear me so I feel as if I am not praying right. Please help me.

Please do not suffer unnecessarily. It is quite odd for a doctor to tell you that pain will last a long time and then offer you no relief. Having said that I do not think that painkillers in the long term will be necessary for you. I will of course do healing for you and I am confident that your pain is already diminishing. You do not have to have faith for healing to work as if it is the right time for suffering to pass it will automatically do so when the healer gets to work.

Please do not feel inadequate when it comes to prayer. God hears us however feeble our attempts at communication. Although we do not necessarily get the answers that we wish for you can be assured that we are heard when we pray.

Some situations are complicated and our suffering is prolonged through no fault of our own. It is very important that you do not see this back pain as a form of punishment and there is no reason for you to feel guilty or ashamed. Certain things remain a mystery and we cannot pretend to understand divine will. But of one thing you can be sure God hears you and your prayer will be answered.

Subject: **Loss Of Mentor**

Aura Soma Bottle # 71 (Jewel in the Lotus- Pink/Clear) will raise your consciousness to connect with the divine. Access to the limitless power of love.

Dear Sarah
I am writing to tell you about my friend aged 25. He has not been the same since our 59-year-old football coach died. This man was popular with the locals and every time we are out my friend says things are not the same without Denis. This happened two years ago.

There is no time limit to grief unfortunately and it is never possible to anticipate the impact of emotional shock. We are all different and process hurt in a unique way. For your friend it is important to be able to reminisce whenever he chooses, even if he has had a few drinks and many months have gone by.

I know you are concerned that he has an unhealthy fixation on Denis, but the man was a mentor and tonic for the troops. So as much as you can support your friend and listen to him. Tell him to kick a ball around regularly in Denis' memory, and to be confident that Denis is still cracking jokes it is just he is not physically present. There is a big pat on the back from Denis, and an assurance that he is not as far away as you would think. A hot Spanish holiday would do you both good, so book that ticket and kick back in celebration of Denis' life and talent.

Subject: **Pregnancy Success**

Aura Soma Bottle # 11 (A Chain of Flowers- Clear/Pink) assists pregnancy.

Dear Sarah
My husband and I have been trying for a baby for five years now. We have just begun our second course of fertility treatment. Will we be successful? Can you offer any tips to help bring the baby along?

First of all, there is quite a lot that can be done on a practical level to ensure pregnancy success. Many couples are "sub-fertile" rather than infertile. This can be due to additives in foods; smoking; too many stimulants like coffee and tea; and contaminated water. Make sure that your diet is of the highest quality. Eat lots of fresh foods, preferably organic, and increase your intake of pure water.

If you think you may have food intolerance please get a blood test from a Clinic which sends samples away for analysis. Also, take a quality vitamin and mineral supplement.

Rose Quartz is a wonderful crystal that increases fertility. Keep a big piece in the bedroom, and if you can wear the power bracelet twenty-four hours a day so much the better.

The Aura Soma bottle, A Chain of Flowers helps support the conception of a child. It is applied to the womb area, and is best kept beside the bed. Make sure you both get plenty of relaxation and fresh air. As with all things that we desperately want, the Universe tends to provide when we let go.

Subject: **Thyroid Problem**

Aura Soma Bottle # 72 (The Clown- Blue/Orange) supports the thyroid function and is the only bottle that will have an impact at a cellular level.

Dear Sarah
I take medication for an under-active thyroid gland that doesn't make me feel any better. There is a lot of stress and tension around the eyes that are often puffy. Also my hair is now almost non-existent. I have tried all types of weird supplements. What should I do to help the situation?

The first thing you should do is to get a blood test to make sure that hormone levels are responding correctly to your medication. Your doctor may need to adjust the way your condition is treated. Your thyroid is clearly under-active. Be careful with supplements.

People with thyroid problems often reach for the kelp tablets. But this can have a detrimental effect. Consult an expert alternative practitioner about this. Kelp can initially cause a surge in iodine levels but fairly quickly it can have an adverse effect and dampen the production of thyroid hormones.

Energetically thyroid problems relate to mother issues. If your mother smothered you with too much attention or was overly protective your thyroid may rebel at the lack of independence! Alternatively if your mother showed any signs of neglect, even in a subtle way, your thyroid has the disposition to become overactive.

Some thyroid conditions alternate between over and under activity. In this instance you may assume that your mother was constantly in your face but lacking in empathy.

Healing of the thyroid may take place with self-reliance and self-acceptance. The gift of unconditional love for your-self and others also helps the energies of the thyroid. You need to know that you are loved so be kind to yourself and expect the best.

Sometimes thyroid problems mean that you should address the issues in your life at a fundamental level. Do you bite your tongue rather than confront people? It is important to speak your truth and seek the positive outcome you are looking for. The majority of people suffering from thyroid problems are women! I wonder why? The best chance of life a thyroid could hope for is a host who knows where they are heading. Do the things you want without guilt, and do not settle for second best. Sleep when you are tired and eat carefully.

Amongst the foods that prevent the body using its available iodine are cabbage, the brassicas, soya, peanuts and maize. Whilst the iodine rich foods are dairy products, bread, cereal, meat and fish. Please find an experienced practitioner before changing your diet drastically.

The crystal Lapis Lazuli supports the throat chakra and Moonstone is a wonderful stone for regulating all hormones. Aura Soma consultants believe that thyroid problems can relate to shock. Bottle no. 72 is particularly recommended. Above all de-stress your life and do not feel guilty about doing so.

Subject: **Suicidal Friend**

Aura Soma Bottle # 48 (Wings of Healing- Violet/Clear) helps someone move beyond suicidal thoughts. Bottle # 78 (Crown Rescue- Violet/Deep Magenta) assists those left behind.

Dear Sarah

I am puzzled by the suicide of my friend. Everything seemed fine for her. She was engaged and had recently enjoyed a holiday abroad. She was in debt but not by more than a grand or two. Why did this happen? I recently went to a fortune-teller but she said nothing about this.

This is clearly a shock for you and for all those who knew your friend. But would it have been helpful to be told of this event in advance? The energies around accidents are hazardous. If someone has made the karmic choice to exit quickly these circumstances make sense. They do not however make sense to those of us who are left behind.

Sometimes a universal understanding of such events appears useless. We just want the loved one back. The lords of karma can keep their agenda to themselves. I do empathise. This is the nature of grief. You have to roll with it. Feel the emotions and respect your friend's decision.

For some reason this action was for her the right thing to do. There is no point in beating yourself up about it. She was in a lot of conflict about her future, and there was to her no way out of debt. She was quite gentle and malleable, and the people around her were chaotic. I think she did not feel known or understood.

There was a generous warmth to her soul, and her environment was too harsh and negative for her. She felt constricted and simply wanted to go home. To be honest she did not anticipate an easy life so the easiest way was out. She was in conflict about her relationship, and nervous about the marriage contract. There was a part of her that wanted the high life or no life at all! She knew she was worth more than the circumstances she found herself in, and she incarnated to affirm that.

Please b assured that she found immediate peace, and she remains close to you. She will be with you now more than previously. She felt stuck, stifled and unhappy. Her life was not her own, so she made this gesture of independence. In so doing she reclaimed her soul and her identity. I know this makes sense to you, because you knew what she was coping with, and you knew the vision she had. Believe me she is now blissful.

Subject: **Panic Attacks**

Aura Soma Bottle # 42 (Harvest- Yellow/Yellow) will ease symptoms of stress.

Dear Sarah
I am very troubled by family worries. My brother had an accident in 1984 that left him with a head injury. Both my Brother's struggle with health problems and we have all had experience of panic attacks. I am afraid of losing my sight. Should we move to the town? Should I learn to drive?

I will be doing healing for your family. I am really sorry to hear of everything you have been through. You are very sweet to worry so much about your brothers. We will see what impact the healing has on their condition. Do let me know. Your Brother's accident has sent a huge shock wave through the family. From time to time this makes you and your brothers susceptible to panics. For yourself the trauma and fear about your eyes has been a huge test. There are few things worse than a threat to your eyesight. I think you are very brave and courageous. Be assured that your eyes are now healthy. I feel the operation was effective.

    You are also doing brilliantly with getting out and about. Again I understand how difficult it can be to lose confidence in that respect. Keep up the good work, and if you ever feel a surge of panic, don't give into it. You have enough confidence now to see that you will be okay.

    You are a survivor. I actually think that learning to drive with bring you more improvements. Make sure all is well with the regulations and get a final eye test. Then proceed with confidence. Driving is good fun and you will learn quite quickly. Relax and be careful, but you have no reason to fear for your own safety. Your learning to drive can lay a lot of family ghosts to rest. Try to leave past trauma behind now, and expect healing to come into your lives. Light a candle for your brothers regularly as this will also help. God bless you all xxx

General Message For Everyone
~ I am so sorry I get inundated with letters, and cannot easily reply to them in person. How-

ever, every letter gets read, and I always do healing work and pray for the situations I read about. If any of you have noticed improvements in your situation do let me know. Or if you have a healing request, you can write and be confident I will be helping you; or rather God will work through me to help you. I do not take credit in any way for the miracles that happen. Make donations to a charity of your choice, or in church if you notice the healing working.

Distance healing is very effective and powerful. I do not need to meet you, so do not panic that you are not being heard. If you need extra help, be sure to write again and keep me posted. I know some people get frustrated that I am not very available for appointments. I hope you will now be assured that I do my very best for all of you within the restrictions of being a human being. Although I cannot literally speak to all of you, I will always remember you in my thoughts and prayers.

If you do need to access a reading at short notice, the best thing to do is to have a look at the web site www.sarahdelamer.com or email me at sarahdelamerehurding@gmail.com. I can help you wherever you are in the world. I do not need to see you face to face in order to affect the energy in your life in a useful way, if you give me permission to do so.

With emergencies and urgent matters email me or phone the mobile on the web site, and leave a message. I will give you help as soon as possible.

Further reading recommended
BY PSYCHIC SARAH

Irene Dalichow and Mike Booth, *Aura Soma: Healing Through Colour, Plant, and Crystal Energy* (USA: Hay House, Inc. 1996).

- Robert Bruce, *Practical Psychic Self-Defense* (Charlottesville: Hampton Roads Publishing Company, Inc. 2002).

- John Drane, *What is The New Age Still Saying To The Church?* (London: Marshall Pickering, 1999).

- Mark Victor Hansen & Robert Allen, *The One Minute Millionaire* (London: Vermilion, 2002).

- Susan Jeffers, *Feel The Fear And Do It Anyway* (London: Arrow, 1991).

- Vicky Wall, *The Miracle of Colour Healing* (London: Thorsons, 1995).

- Alma Daniel, Timothy Wyllie, & Andrew Ramer, *Ask Your Angels* (London: Piatkus, 1995)

- Melody, *Love is in the Earth- A Kaleidoscope of Crystals Updated* (USA: Earth-Love publishing, 1997).

- Geddes MacGregor, *Reincarnation in Christianity* (Illinois: Quest Books, 1989).

- Roger Hurding, *Pathways To Wholeness- Pastoral Care in a Postmodern Age* (London: Hodder & Stoughton, 1998).

- Linda Goodman, *Star Signs* (London: Pan Books, 1988).

- Toshu Fukami, *Lucky Fortune- 4 basic principles to make fortune roll your way* (London: Thorsons, 2000).

Dear Psychic Sarah

Acknowledgments

Endless gratitude to The Irish Nation, which it has been my pleasure to serve for so many years with mystical, spiritual, and psychic insights. My heart will always be in Ireland, even as my spirit and soul roam the world and the ethers.

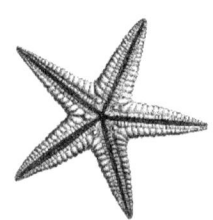

www.ingramcontent.com/pod-product-compliance
Lightning Source LLC
Chambersburg PA
CBHW071158160426
43196CB00011B/2114